Anonymous

Music and Moonlight

Poems and Songs

Anonymous

Music and Moonlight
Poems and Songs

ISBN/EAN: 9783744712477

Printed in Europe, USA, Canada, Australia, Japan

Cover: Foto ©Thomas Meinert / pixelio.de

More available books at **www.hansebooks.com**

MUSIC AND MOONLIGHT

POEMS AND SONGS

BY

ARTHUR O'SHAUGHNESSY

London
CHATTO AND WINDUS, PUBLISHERS
1874

CONTENTS.

A

CONTENTS.

ODE.

WE are the music makers,
  And we are the dreamers of dreams,
Wandering by lone sea-breakers,
  And sitting by desolate streams ;—
World-losers and world-forsakers,
  On whom the pale moon gleams :
Yet we are the movers and shakers
  Of the world for ever, it seems.

With wonderful deathless ditties
We build up the world's great cities,
  And out of a fabulous story
  We fashion an empire's glory :

One man with a dream, at pleasure,
　　Shall go forth and conquer a crown ;
And three with a new song's measure
　　Can trample a kingdom down.

We, in the ages lying
　　In the buried past of the earth,
Built Nineveh with our sighing,
　　And Babel itself in our mirth ;
And o'erthrew them with prophesying
　　To the old of the new world's worth ;
For each age is a dream that is dying,
　　Or one that is coming to birth.

A breath of our inspiration
Is the life of each generation ;
　　A wondrous thing of our dreaming
　　Unearthly, impossible seeming—
The soldier, the king, and the peasant
　　Are working together in one,

Till our dream shall become their present,

And their work in the world be·done.

They had no vision amazing

Of the goodly house they are raising;

They had no divine foreshowing

Of the land to which they are going:

But on one man's soul it hath broken,

A light that doth not depart;

And his look, or a word he hath spoken,

Wrought flame in another man's heart.

And therefore to-day is thrilling

With a past day's late fulfilling;

‘ And the multitudes are enlisted

In the faith that their fathers resisted,

And, scorning the dream of to-morrow,

Are bringing to pass, as they may,

In the world, for its joy or its sorrow,

The dream that was scorned yesterday.

But we, with our dreaming and singing,
  Ceaseless and sorrowless we !
The glory about us clinging
  Of the glorious futures we see,
Our souls with high music ringing :
  O men ! it must ever be
That we dwell, in our dreaming and singing,
  A little apart from ye.

For we are afar with the dawning
  And the suns that are not yet high,
And out of the infinite morning
  Intrepid you hear us cry—
How, spite of your human scorning,
  Once more God's future draws nigh,
And already goes forth the warning
  That ye of the past must die.

Great hail ! we cry to the comers
  From the dazzling unknown shore ;

Bring us hither your sun and your summers,

And renew our world as of yore ;

You shall teach us your song's new numbers,

And things that we dreamed not before :

Yea, in spite of a dreamer who slumbers,

And a singer who sings no more.

MUSIC AND MOONLIGHT.

"A tone
Of some world far from ours,
Whose music and moonlight and feeling
Are one."

SHELLEY.

MUSIC AND MOONLIGHT.

OH, lovely, prisoned soul of Eucharis !
 I knew your sorrow and I felt your bliss.
I was not rich Sir John you used to hate,
Nor stupid smiling D'Arcy, nor that loud
Intolerable fool whose empty prate
Enchanted all the girls, nor of their crowd,
Your hopeless speechless lovers, who had
   vowed
Unutterable nothings with their eyes
As often as you passed them : all I know
You hated, laughed, or yawned at. I was
   wise,
And never wooed you ; nay, indeed, although

I had the very secret of your soul,

I seldom spoke to you.   One brilliant night,

When the great drawing-room was full of light,

And dizzy with the rustling of a whole

Sweet restless ocean of bright silk and gauze,

In an uncertain, half delirious pause,

While many an eye was suddenly o'er-brimmed

With softened light'ning, that till then had dimmed

Never its glittering opal,—Eucharis,

You played.   There was a faint subsiding hiss

For silence, then your grand piano's tone

Grew to a wonderful voice, became your own—

Spoke, prayed, sang, wept, and died away at
        last,

Far away in a silver dream that past

Back to your soul's fair heaven ;—and I alone,

A poet silent near the crowded door,

Had heard your soul and understood and known ;

And, as you ended, overcome once more

With sadness there was no accounting for—

A sadness known alike to me and you—

I went away, and dreamed the next day through.

'Twas after midnight, and the house was dim

And full of mysteries ; late, a costly glare

Guided the mazy steps of many a slim

And high-born beauty through the chambers fair,

And out to glittering corridor and stair,

Made marvellous with marble luxuries .

And rich exotic glowing motionless ;

Now there were blue and shadowy presences

Gliding impalpable in bluer gloom ;

A myriad were the memories in each room

That met all noiselessly ; the antique Past

A minuet was dancing with the last

Still faintly blushing spectre of that eve,

Whose perfumed rose lay dying on the floor :

Some shadows seemed to laugh, and some to grieve,

As the blue moonlight fell on them from door

And distant window ; but a step once more

Disturbed unwontedly their silent spells,

And such a fragrant warmth the still air bore

As subtly to those jaded shadows tells

Of one with living thrilling heart a-nigh ;

Then shadowy, half arrayed, with moonlit eye,

And face amazed in an unweary dream,

Pale Lady Eucharis came back alone,

And found that gold-hung, curtained room was
   grown

Again a wide sweet desert, where the gleam   ·

Of vacillating stars might penetrate,

And the moon's pallid taper fingers played

With all the scarce-seen marvelries that stayed

. In the strange fitful glimmer.   There did wait

Her weird-toned sweet piano, open still,

Eloquent in the silence, with fair thrill

Living in every long-drawn golden chord

That reached far darkness and far mystery.

So she sat down, and touched the white keyboard,

Drawing therefrom a wonderful faint sigh,

Whereto another fainter made reply;

And then it was as though some distant sea

Were opening all its soft heart tenderly

To coral flower and fair anemone,

And long sweet amber waves were passing by,

And sirens' songs were floating from blue isles

Where dreams may be for ever; and, at whiles,

The music seemed to be all made of smiles,

Wide soft illuminations of the soul.

So Eucharis played on, until her whole

Unearthly dream-world came about her fair,

And every thought, transfigured, seemed some

    rare '

Ethereal flower, that did transform the air

With element of perfume exquisite.

Then, unto her, enchanted in that dim

Enchanted chamber,—lured by the delight

Of some arpeggio's murmur, or the slight

Immortal fantasy of some frail rhythm,—

There came the lovely spirit even of him

Whom all her soul loved—Chopin, magical,

Seraphic, enigmatic, deathless,—yea,

And took her on strange voyaging far away

In a sweet silver bark o'er mystical

Melodious waves beneath the moon's strange ray.

It was a golden, night-illumined stream

That bore them on, where many a topaz star

Shot down some brilliant and unwonted beam,

And here and there great lakes of nenuphar

And lustrous lotos glimmered.   And they passed

High gardens, where the freed souls of all flowers

Talked magically, and blue river bowers,

Where sirens slept and moaned ; and all at last

The yellow flood grew narrow, and the shore,

Closing in steeply on them, more and more

Loomed with tremendous temples, marble massed

On marble, water-steps and peristyles,

And bare, sheer side of building windowless,

From whose high terrace stooped the pendant palms.

And then they entered long and winding aisles,

The amber water beating with soft stress

Slim lurid pillars, through whose long defiles

They floated : deepest luxuries and calms

Immeasurable and perfumes filled those ways ;

Also lone memories of delicious days

No man hath written of fell there like balms

On Eucharis, till pleasure came in tears,

And her soul lived above life's days and years.

Lo ! now, the dusky splendours of a fane,

And priests long watching, watching long in

    vain,

For the sweet coming of some thing foretold,

Some miracle believed in as of old,

Some momentary heaven, or exquisite

Rarest reflowering of the lifted soul.

The wonders of a dim roof overwrit

With mystic star-signs, like a mighty scroll,

Are darkened by vague incense clouds that roll

Tremendous, rising from strange censers lit

With fragrant flames before grand gods, who sit

Moveless, gigantic, in the eternal peace

And silence of the soul for ever found.

And lo! a place where praying hath no sound, ·

And incense fails—while ecstasies release

The o'erwrought spirit of one lovely youth

Alone, above the world.   The sky, in truth,

Is nearer than the shadow of the earth ;

And the ethereal blue, inscrutable,

Is working there a mystery, that birth

And death were not akin to.   Mutable,

The lurid, low, adjacent stars draw nigh,

And open splendidly as each floats by—

A glittering inner garden full of hues

And liquid singing, and great wealthy shower

Of perfumes, that descend 'mid glowing dews,

Dyeing the night's wide lifted azure flower ;

And lo! in the remote, unearthly space,

One new star, wonderful with pallid fire

And plumage like a rainbow.   Then the place

Where that lone youth, with fair ecstatic face,

Lies fainting in the soul's supreme desire,

Becometh full of radiance ; the keen light

Of yon far apparition strikes it fair,

And haloeth all its mysteries in rare

Intense transfigurement.   And soon : " To-night,"

That fair one singeth, rising glorified—

" To-night the hundred years of yearning cease ;

The Phœnix hath the Aloe flower for bride :

To-night he cometh ; and the soul hath peace,

And lovely consummation and release ! "

Oh, what a melody his high voice made,

Floating down like clear silver ! and each
    priest,

Waiting beneath, in mystic garb arrayed,

Echoed the echo to his fellow-priest,

Till the last told it to each man who prayed,

And to the sacred bird and sacred beast,

And to the thirsting earth, and to the Nile,

Moaning down many a waveless, yellow mile.

Most sweet light fell upon each distant isle,

And on green granite and red porphyry,

On all the temples and the terraces,

On all the gardens and the palaces;

And avenues of sphinxes made reply

Of rich Memnonic music, rosily

Glowing beneath the green acacia-trees.

Beyond the desert and the Atlas Mountains

There is a garden full of flowers and fountains,

An unknown labyrinth, for ever lifted

Out of the world : there, soul by soul hath drifted

On buoyant, mystic tides of rapturous dreaming;

And youths and women lie there, lovely seeming,

In rich exuberant posture, their eyes shaded

By some pale bloom, their beauty nothing faded

Through untold decades of enchanted sleeping,

Lulled by some sweet illusion which the weeping

Of those enchanted waters still is keeping

Dreamy accordance with. And there, high glowing,

Exalted above every creature's knowing,

Rapt and unfaltering for a hundred years,

The Phœnix watches for the Aloe's blowing,

Singing strange songs until the Aloe hears.

    Desolate, dreary,

    The world was, and weary

      The soul was of sighing

      With no soul replying,

    With no love to hallow

      Lone living and dying,

    Till it dreamed of thee, Aloe—

      Beautiful Aloe !

    Then the soul bore thee

    Where dreams might adore thee,

Past island and bower
And amber Nile-shallow :
　Aloe, my flower,
　One living hour
I shall live for thee—
　Aloe, my Aloe !

Aloe, I made thee
A garden to shade thee,
　Where moonlight is falling,
Pale, soothful, and sallow ;
And there, with the gleam of thee,
I, in my dream of thee,
　Yearn for thee, calling
　　Aloe, my Aloe !

All the rare blisses
The lost world misses,
　Such have I found for thee,
Aloe, my Aloe !

Sweet sight and sound for thee,

All lying bound for thee,

Wait my soul's kisses,

Beautiful Aloe !

All the strange riches

That green sea-witches

Bury and hide

In the coral niches,

I have gleaned them from tide

And cavern and shallow,

To be for my bride,

Beautiful Aloe!

A soul of a maiden

With music laden

Shall serve thee and bring to thee,

Aloe, my Aloe !

Each treasure of Aden,

Each perfect thing to thee,

C

Whereof I sing to thee,
Beautiful Aloe !

The soul is turning
To unearthly yearning,
The heart is burning,
    Aloe, my Aloe !
With love whose learning
    Leaves no glad returning,
Wert thou beyond earning—
    Beautiful Aloe !

Fade away faces
In life's past places ;
    Stay for me only,
    Aloe, my Aloe !
Wonder that graces
The rare dream spaces
    Where the soul walks lonely—
        Beautiful Aloe !

And Chopin and fair Lady Eucharis,

Lost in a moonlit miracle of bliss,

Were walking 'midst of mazy trellises

Through the unearthly garden of the Aloe,

With many coloured magic glimmering;

Fair monstrous flowers, of midnight's fostering,

Opened in some blue evanescent halo,

And shed their odorous secret, languishing

In hectic tremulous raptures; mystic loves

Were mingling their eternities in words

Unknown, and mellower than low notes of doves :

But more than all the flowers and the birds,

With endless outpour of enchanted song·

The high rapt Phœnix filled the place with long

Luxurious ecstasy; the strange trees sighed,

And waved their quaint leaves to the passionate

    measure;

The fountains rose like phantoms glorified,

And momently, as with some thrill of pleasure,

Doubled the fluent music of their tide;

· Until at length, with most melodious thunder

Of many a veil-like petal rent asunder,

There issued to the moonlight a slim wonder,—

The amber Spirit of the Aloe flower,

To fill the rich life of one midnight hour.

Fair and unearthly was She, ravishing

One brief exalted moment, like the rare

Frail-shapen love of visions, or the thing

Divinely fabled, making lone life fair,

And poignant death a passionate triumphing.

Then a new spell, and all is vanishing,

And all that garden's magic seems afar

In ancient buried ages ; only awhile,

Faint over waves, or dwindling through wide mile

Of voyage ethereal, or from some calm star

Cast with sweet echo, comes in mystic wise

The Aloe's singing ere the Phœnix dies :—

Once in a hundred years

Thou shalt forget thy tears,

. And all thy life shall flower

Into one infinite hour.

If thou wilt flee the bliss

Of each dull earthly kiss,

Then thou shalt joy like this

Once in a hundred years.

Once in a hundred years

Such voice as no man hears

Shall charm thy spirit, sighing,

With more than song's replying.

If thou wilt never seek

Earth's love-notes false and weak,

Then thou shalt hear me speak

Once in a hundred years.

Once in a hundred years

Sorrows and hopes and fears

Shall free thy spirit, thrilling,

In joy's supreme fulfilling.

If thou hast never placed

A wish on life's drear waste,

Then rapture shalt thou taste

Once in a hundred years.

Once in a hundred years

Thy soul its Eden nears,

The fair star richly ringing

With thine exalted singing.

If thou wilt never tire,

But in all thy song aspire,

Divine shall throb thy lyre

Once in a hundred years.

Once in a hundred years

Life's darkness from thee clears,

And high and God-like seeming

Beneath thy skies of dreaming.

If, through all dreary grieving,

Thy soul went on believing,

Bright shall be thine achieving

Once in a hundred years.

Once in a hundred years

Lone life a blossom bears ;

The pale leaves break asunder,

And lo! how sweet a wonder !

If worlds of men were glad

While thou wert alway sad,

High joy thou shalt have had

Once in a hundred years.

Once in a hundred years,

Wonderful to thine ears,

My silver voice, descending,

With thy deep soul is blending ;

Yea, if thou didst disdain,

And hold man's soothing vain,

And lived to hear my strain

Once in a hundred years.

Once in a hundred years

Of bliss shall be thy tears ;

Yea, if thou ne'er didst borrow

Of earthly sweet or sorrow;

Yea, if thy soul forsakes

Dull joys, and purely takes

The ecstasy that wakes

Once in a hundred years.

The blue cupolas of a silent town

Rise golden-spiked and glittering to the moon ;

And in one latticed chamber, looking down

On sleepless, murmuring Euphrates, strewn

With shrouded barks, an Odalisc, unseen,

Splendidly couched on piled-up cushions green,

And damask and gold-broidered, sighs one sigh,

And gazing far into the warm blue sky,
Sings softly, as she sings when none is nigh.

Am I not princess great?
One whom a god men rate
Loves me, and gives me state
    Over all queens:
Yea, but I am not glad ;
Something no man hath had
Lives in me lone and sad ;
Bulbul, whose heart is mad,
    Knows what it means.

Waste away, golden hair ;
Fade away, face so fair ;
Are you, then, all men care
    To have or win ?
Fade ! you were bought and sold ;
Die ! and free what you hold,
Unknown, unthought, untold,

Form like the cage of gold
Bulbul is in.

Oh ! to be there afar,
Free as my thoughts now are,
Joying in yon green star,
   So pure, so high !
Free under silver beams,
Free by enchanted streams,
Singing and dreaming dreams,
   Bulbul and I !

There I should find the red
Souls of the roses dead
Living again, and wed
   To Bulbuls sweet ;
There I should see my love,
My own, my sweet, my dove :
He should be heaven above,
   I earth at his feet.

Then it would not seem miles

Out to the emerald isles

Set in the shining smiles

Far in blue sea ;

I should be there as soon

As the white birds at noon,

Blue night and golden moon

Rising o'er me.

Would I were free to cling,

Faint bird or unseen thing,

To a ship's gleaming wing,

Far, far away !

All is so fair, I know—

Once a song told me so—

There where the white ships go,

There I would stay.

Sing to me, captive bird,

Strange song or foreign word,

Such as I oft have heard
　　You sing or sigh ;
　I am a captive too,
　Loving yon heaven so blue,
　And, on earth, only you—
　　Longing to die !

And Bulbul sang a strangely woven song,
So tender and so deep; it was not long
Ere, sighing once again, that lady fell
Into a painless sleep beneath its spell ;
And then indeed he set her chained soul free,　.
And flew away with it ;—no Bulbul he—
But Prince of that same green enchanted star
Whose palaces and gardens gleamed afar
In magic coruscation through the night.

And still wide-launched upon a wandering wave
Of evanescent music, new delight
Allured the lifted spirit on to rave
Through shifting scenes ; and many a structure slight,

Amazingly consummate, shone divine

With momentary beauty in the fine

Impalpable, unearthly fashioning

Of elevated fantasy.   Clear wing

Of wordless thought angelic urged alone

That ether immaterial ; and the sighs

Of some enchanted passion dimly known

Filled it with blissful yearnings and replies

In rich enormous cadence : lofty chants

Broke in with wild illusion shadowy ;

Grand joy, that for no bounded utterance pants,

Lived on in clear acclaim, and, like a sea

Hushed beneath glimmering moonlight evermore,

All rich, all precious melancholy bore

Its dim unravished secret under smile

And rapt melodious silence.   Then awhile

That subtle sweet magician, with his spell

Of supernatural dreaming, took the soul

Of Eucharis, in whom no thought did dwell,

No grief, no painful fretting, that might tell

Of dull embodied being's hard control,

And set it in one place, that, through the whole

Spoiled Eden of the earth, is loveliest,

Loneliest, most divine ; no people's feet

Do ever interrupt its trance of rest ;

And in the moonlight, crowning all its hill

Like an unearthly halo, shone the sweet,

The pure Alhambra, with the Moor's look still

Abiding on it.   Holy seemed the hour

In that immortal dream-work ivory aisled,

The changeless paradise of bird and flower,

And perfumed mystery and echoes wild,

Haunted by some Æolian soul whose sighs

Ravish the golden days with the surprise

Of fabulous wandering music.   Now the moon

Poured down her unchecked splendour there, and

    reigned

Supreme, ecstatic in a radiant swoon

O'er all that alabaster palace stained

With legendary fantasies : her beam

Showered the spectral glory of a dream

On slim phantasmal fountains whispering,

And touched with her most soft transfiguring

The flowering oleanders in their sleep,

And many a fair unruffled flower-heap,

Filling a ruinous window with its flame.

There might the soul exalted make a home

With thought's lone rhapsody, to ever roam

The exquisite desolation, till death came

In most refined way supernatural,

Of overwhelming perfume's rich excess,

Or music's long dissolving charm ; unless

The moon's unfaltering glamour made one fall

Into the wide amaze of endless trance,

Or some weird spell of things unknown by chance

Brought an immortal madness.   But, behold !

There was a mystery of speech throughout

That moon-hushed labyrinth of lovely ways :

The thin pilasters and the roof-work cold,

Like frozen pointed fringe-work wrought about

Each dreamy corridor, and—where wan rays

Of moonlight fingered their enigma, set

In many gleaming amethyst and jet,

Topaz and jasper, and carbuncle stone—

The quaint rich azulejos, with their own

Melodious manner of bright metaphor,

Intricate through zigzagging arabesque—

All joined in mystic utterance, and bore

One meaning : 'Twas the same thing Chopin said

Once in a dream, and murmured o'er and o'er

In music, and the world hath no speech for :

The Bulbul sang it to the Odalisc ;

The Aloe and the Phœnix, as they wed,

Sang it in joy the earth no longer owned :

It was the mystic thing priest showed to priest,

And pale Memnonic sphinxes slow intoned ;

And the waves' echo of it hath not ceased.

Then, further, being in that place so sweet

Above all other in the world, it seemed

That Chopin's soul and Eucharis did meet;

Yea, that he spoke now as she never dreamed,

Asking her spirit if she would not choose

To be henceforth where never need she lose

That fair illuminated vision's height,

Hearing his speech in all its clear delight,

Where those exalted creatures joyed alway,

Her soul's true sisters? Then, she said not Yea,

But with intense emotion inward spoke.

And therewith something burst asunder—broke!

Down in that shrouded chamber far away

The grand piano snapt one string; but oh,

Pale Lady Eucharis fell back, as though

Her dream grew deeper; and, at dawn of day,

They found her—dead; as one asleep she lay!

SONG.

I MADE another garden, yea,
  For my new love ;
I left the dead rose where it lay,
  And set the new above.
Why did the summer not begin?
  Why did my heart not haste?
My old love came and walked therein,
  And laid the garden waste.

She entered with her weary smile,
  Just as of old ;
She looked around a little while,
  And shivered at the cold.

Her passing touch was death to all,
Her passing look a blight :
She made the white rose-petals fall,
And turned the red rose white.

Her pale robe, clinging to the grass,
Seemed like a snake
That bit the grass and ground, alas !
And a sad trail did make.
She went up slowly to the gate ;
And there, just as of yore,
She turned back at the last to wait,
And say farewell once more.

SONG.

HAS summer come without the rose,
  Or left the bird behind?
Is the blue changed above thee,
  O world! or am I blind?
Will you change every flower that grows,
  Or only change this spot,
Where she who said, I love thee,
  Now says, I love thee not?

The skies seemed true above thee,
  The rose true on the tree;
The bird seemed true the summer through,
  But all proved false to me.

World ! is there one good thing in you,

    Life, love, or death—or what ?

Since lips that sang, I love thee,

    Have said, I love thee not?

I think the sun's kiss will scarce fall

    Into one flower's gold cup ;

I think the bird will miss me,

    And give the summer up.

O sweet place ! desolate in tall

    Wild grass, have you forgot

How her lips loved to kiss me,

    Now that they kiss me not ?

Be false or fair above me,

    Come back with any face,

Summer !—do I care what you do ?

    You cannot change one place—

The grass, the leaves, the earth, the dew,

The grave I make the spot—

Here, where she used to love me,

Here, where she loves me not.

SONG.

I WENT to her who loveth me no more,
 And prayed her bear with me, if so she might ;
For I had found day after day too sore,
 And tears that would not cease night after night.
And so I prayed her, weeping, that she bore
To let me be with her a little ; yea,
 To soothe myself a little with her sight,
Who loved me once, ah ! many a night and day.

Then she who loveth me no more, maybe
 She pitied somewhat : and I took a chain
To bind myself to her, and her to me ;
 Yea, so that I might call her mine again.

Lo! she forbade me not; but I and she

Fettered her fair limbs, and her neck more fair,

    Chained the fair wasted white of love's domain,

And put gold fetters on her golden hair.

Oh! the vain joy it is to see her lie

    Beside me once again; beyond release,

Her hair, her hand, her body, till she die,

    All mine, for me to do with as I please!

For, after all, I find no chain whereby

To chain her heart to love me as before,

    Nor fetter for her lips, to make them cease

From saying still she loveth me no more.

SONG.

SHE has gone wandering, wandering away;
   Very sad madness hath taken her to-day.
Would I might hold her by her hair's golden mass,
By her two feet, her girdle, her whole self in the
      glass
Of the years past, that change not, though she change
      and stray.

For twain were we no more, to love and to pass;
For she hath both our heavens, and God heard her
      say
Fair oaths that but curse both for ever, if, alas!
            She hath gone wandering away.

Shall not some memory—nothing I can say—

Soon or late plead with her more than I pray?

Shall not some song, more than my singing hath?

Yea, O God! let me find her, though dying in the

grass;

Ere she die let me hold her, and forget how to-day

She hath gone wandering away.

MAY.

DREAM-LIKE glow of a rapt noon hour,
   Rose-tinted rapture, that may not last,
Heaven seen clear between shower and shower,
   Dawn colour ruined by day's overcast—
How shall I sing of the maid called May?
How shall I sing of the year's supreme flower?
   Fading away, ah! fading away,
   Fading, fading away!

Maiden May was a white snow bloom,
   A wan white lily wearily fair;

Summer her death was, and summer her doom ;

In love her garden, and love her air,

She grew and paled in the full red ray,

A lily that stood in the rose's room,

Fading away, ah ! fading away,

Fading, fading away !

Her head was haloed with strange, sweet gold ;

Sadder than life is, and high as life's dream ;

Her lifted face, lit manifold

With the inner eyes' transcendant gleam,

Was like the fair lit face of a day

Filled with the azure it may not hold,

Fading away, ah ! fading away,

Fading, fading away !

She walked one eve beneath the trees

Who may forget her slender grace ?

Lingering, gliding with soft ease,
  Singing fair thoughts in that fair place,
Seeming at length, in mystic gray
The angel some fond dreamer sees,
  Fading away, ah ! fading away,
  Fading, fading away !

No empress ever in all men's sight
  Moved with a loftier splendid look
Than May did, making summer bright,
  Till our sad summer she forsook ;
Then a white saint it was that lay
Upon a couch all clad in white,
  Fading away, ah ! fading away,
  Fading, fading away !

But how shall a song of mine avail
  To sing of the wondrous hidden soul,
That stronger grew as the form grew frail,
  Until it passed from the form's control ?

She rose—the form is no longer May,

But a fair wan flower, fallen and pale,

Fading away, yes, fading away,

Fading, fading away !

PROPHETIC BIRDS.

ON May-morn two lovers stood
 For the first time in the wood ;
And lip wooed lip, and heart wooed heart,
Till words must cease, and tears must start ;
And overhead in the rustling green
The birds talked over their fate unseen.

'Sure,' said the thrush, 'we'll wed them soon ;'
'Yea,' said the turtle-dove, 'in June ;'
'They'll make fine sport ere the year is out,'
Said the magpie between a laugh and a shout.
And heedlessly the lovers heard
The senseless babble of bird with bird.

'Sure,' croaked the jackdaw, 'in July
They'll quarrel, or no daw am I—
Why, let them, since they are but men;'
'They can make it up though,' quoth the wren.
And heedlessly the lovers heard
A senseless babble of bird with bird.

'Love with them shall be sweet, ere sad,'
Said the goldfinch,—'August shall make them glad.'
'Yea,' said the oriole, 'one rich noon
They shall lengthen love in a golden swoon.'
And all this while the lovers heard
But a senseless babble of bird with bird.

'My news is from Prince Popinjay,'
Sighed the hoopoe. 'Ah! one August day
They shall dream in the sunset, and fall asleep,
And one shall awake from the dream to weep.'
And heedlessly the lovers heard
This senseless babble of bird with bird.

E

But a nightingale in a far-off shade

That moment silenced the chattering glade,

And sang like an angel from above

Some mystic song of eternal love.

And all this singing the lovers heard

As the senseless babble of bird with bird.

SONG.

LOVE took three gifts and came to greet
　　My heart : Love gave me what he had,
The first thing sweet, the second sweet,
　　And the last thing sweet and sad.

The first thing was a lily wan,
　　The second was a rose full red,
The third thing was my lady-swan,
　　My lady-love here lying dead.

Come and kiss us, come and see
How Love hath wrought with her and me ;
　　Over our grave the years shall creep,
　　Under the years we two shall sleep.

SONG OF BETROTHAL.

O SISTER-SOUL and lover,
　　Mine to eternity,
Whom dreams and hopes discover
Where dreamed-of heavens may be !
Those nights the skies are glass,
Those days the skies are blue,
　　Do you quite near me pass ?
Do I draw near to you?

　　Those days I listen vainly
To sounds the skies let fall ;
I never catch a word, and yet
It seems I hear you call.

Those nights I see quite plainly,
O sister-soul and lover !
My heaven through many a fair inlet,
And you, who fill it all.

O sister-soul and lover,
Mine to eternity,
Whom heart and thoughts discover
In climes remote from me !
The south wind that brings summer,
The amber-laden sea,
The bird, the rarest comer,
Bring these no word from thee ?

I think I see you under
Strange palms with leaves of gold ;
Your foreign dress, and in your hand
The quaint bright fan you hold :
I sit sometimes and wonder,
O sister mine, and lover,

What ship shall bring you from your land,

To me here in the cold ?

 O lover mine and sister,

 That lady you must be

 My soul once knew, then missed her

 A whole eternity.

My soul, still pining, fretting,

Feels all your memory;

 O mine beyond forgetting,

Canst thou remember me?

 I think we sang together,

Bright songs, whose words yet cling

Divinely to my lips, and quite

Their music with them bring :

 They tell of fairer weather,

 O lady mine, and lover ;

I write them down, and as I write,

I think I hear you sing.

O sister mine and lover,

Buried and lost to me,

Whose grave my tears discover,

Where'er thy grave may be :

Art buried where the grass is,

And flowers that were like thee,

Where my foot sometimes passes ?

Or is your grave the sea ?

Wherever you are sleeping,

Indeed though o'er your head

You see dark waves of dismal blue,

And wet weed is your bed ;

O you must feel my weeping,

Yea, sister mine and lover ;

I will not take my love from you,

Nor think that you are dead.

O angel bride and sister,

My heart knows thou art she,

Whom lips that never kissed her
Shall kiss eternally.
When heaven is quite a glass
And love sees through and through,
How shall sick longing pass,
And my soul rush to you!

These shall not be for ever,
Days, nights, and darkness sore,
Drear time that seems a shoreless sea,
And death that owns no shore;
Then what shall stay or sever,
O angel love and sister,
Thy soul from mine or me from thee,
My bride for evermore?

SONG OF PALMS.

MIGHTY, luminous, and calm
   Is the country of the palm,
Crowned with sunset and sunrise,
Under blue unbroken skies,
Waving from green zone to zone,
Over wonders of its own;
Trackless, untraversed, unknown,
   Changeless through the centuries.

Who can say what thing it bears?
   Blazing bird and blooming flower,

Dwelling there for years and years,

  Hold the enchanted secret theirs :

Life and death and dream have made

Mysteries in many a shade,

Hollow haunt and hidden bower

Closed alike to sun and shower.

Who is ruler of each race

Living in each boundless place,

  Growing, flowering, and flying,

  Glowing, revelling, and dying?

Wave-like, palm by palm is stirred,

And the bird sings to the bird,

And the day sings one rich word,

  And the great night comes replying.

Long red reaches of the cane,

Yellow winding water-lane,

Verdant isle and amber river,

Lisp and murmur back again,

And ripe under-worlds deliver

Rapturous souls of perfume, hurled

Up to where green oceans quiver

In the wide leaves' restless world.

Like a giant led astray

Seemeth each effulgent day,

Wandering amazed and lonely

Up and down each forest way,

Lured by bird and charmed by bloom,

Lulled to sleep by great perfume,

Knowing, marvelling, and only

Bearing some rich dream away.

Many thousand years have been,

And the sun alone hath seen,

Like a high and radiant ocean,

All the fair palm world in motion ;

But the crimson bird hath fed

With its mate of equal red,

And the flower in soft explosion

With the flower hath been wed.

And its long luxuriant thought

Lofty palm to palm hath taught,

While a single vast liana

All one brotherhood hath wrought,

Crossing forest and savannah,

Binding fern and coco-tree,

Fig-tree, buttress-tree, banana,

Dwarf cane and tall marití.

And no sun hath reached the rock

Shaken by loud water shock,

Where with flame-like plumage flutter
Golden birds in glaring flock,
Bright against the darkness utter,
Lighting up the solitude,
Where dim cascades roar and mutter
Through the river's foaming feud.

And beyond the trees are scant,
And a hidden lake is lying
Under wide-leaved water-plant,
Blossom with white blossom vying.
Who shall say what thing is heard,
Who shall say what liquid word,
Caught by the bentivi bird,
Over lake and blossom flying?

All around and overhead,
Spells of splendid change are shed ;

Who shall tell enchanted stories
Of the forests that are dead ?
Lo ! the soul shall grow immense,
Looking on strange hues intense,
Gazing at the flaunted glories
Of the hundred-coloured lories.

OUTCRY.

IN all my singing and speaking,
   I send my soul forth seeking :
O soul of my soul's dreaming,
   When wilt thou hear and speak ?
Lovely and lonely seeming,
Thou art there in my dreaming ;
Hast thou no sorrow for speaking?
   Hast thou no dream to seek?

In all my thinking and sighing,
   In all my desolate crying,
I send my heart forth yearning,
   O heart that mayst be nigh!

Like a bird weary of flying,

My heavy heart, returning,

Bringeth me no replying,

   Of word, or thought, or sigh.

In all my joying and grieving,

   Living, hoping, believing,

I send my love forth flowing,

   To find my unknown love.

O world that I am leaving,

O heaven where I am going,

Is there no finding and knowing,

   Around, within, or above? ·

O soul of my soul's seeing,

   O heart of my heart's being,

O love of dreaming and waking

   And living and dying for—

Out of my soul's last aching,

Out of my heart just breaking—

Doubting, falling, forsaking,

I call on you this once more.

Are you too high or too lowly

To come at length unto me?

Are you too sweet or too holy

For me to have and to see?

Wherever you are, I call you,

Ere the falseness of life enthral you,

Ere the hollow of death appal you,

While yet your spirit is free.

Have you not seen, in sleeping,

A lover that might not stay,

And remembered again with weeping,

And thought of him through the day?—

Ah! thought of him long and dearly,

Till you seemed to behold him clearly,

And could follow the dull time merely

With heart and love far away?

F

Have you not known him kneeling

　To a deathless vision of you,

Whom only an earth was concealing,

　Whom all that was heaven proved true?

O surely some wind gave motion

To his words like a wave of the ocean;

Ay! so that you felt his devotion,

　And smiled, and wondered, and knew.

And what are you thinking and saying,

　In the land where you are delaying?

Have you a chain to sever?

　Have you a prison to break?

O love! there is one love for ever,

And never another love—never;

And hath it not reached you, my praying

　And singing these years for your sake?

We two, made one, should have power

　To grow to a beautiful flower,

A tree for men to sit under

Beside life's flowerless stream :

But I without you am only

A dreamer, fruitless and lonely ;

And you without me, a wonder

In my most beautiful dream.

AZURE ISLANDS.

SHIPMEN, sailing by night and day,
    High on the azure sea,
Do you not meet upon your way,
    Joyous and swift and free,
Sailing, sailing, ever sailing,
    Nigh to the western skylands,
My soul, a bark beyond your hailing,
    Bound for the azure islands?

My soul is like a shining bird
    Skimming the crested spray,
And singing, singing—have you not heard?—
    Along the azure way ;

It voyages like a cloudlet growing
  Out of the sky and ocean,
A buoyant rapturous film all glowing,
  And freighted with emotion.

When halcyon spells are on the wave
  And in the enchanted sight,
A path the dappling sunbeams pave
  Grows to intensest light;
And down in blue dominions, vainly
  Now the sea-sprite's wonder;
The sunken cities glitter plainly,
  And murmur in hushed thunder:

When every little billow breaks
  Into a liquid bloom,
And sings for one changed soul that wakes,
  Glad in so sweet a tomb;
And when in the rich horizon's dimness,
  Over the ocean revel,

Some blue land with a palm's crowned slimness
  Looms at the sea waves' level :

Then my elated bark, my soul,
  Speeds rapturously, and seems
A cloud body at my control
  To realise my dreams ;
And onward, drawing nearer, nearer,
  To western deepening skylands,
With ever a higher, yea, and dearer,
  Dream of the azure islands—

I reach them as the wave wanes low,
  Leaving its stranded ores,
And evening floods of amber glow
  And sleep around their shores ;
Then, with a bird's will, a wind's power,
  My soul dwells there ecstatic,
Knowing each palm-tree and each flower,
  Gorgeous and enigmatic.

It plunges through some perfumed brake,

Or depth of odorous shade,

That walls and roofs a dim hushed lak e,

Where endless dreams have stayed ;

And there it takes the incarnation

Of some amphibious blossom,

And lies in long-drawn contemplation,

Buoyed on the water's bosom ;

And mingling in the mysteries

Of interchanging hues,

And songs and sighs and silences,

That in one magic fuse ;

My soul my solitude enriches

Through that profuse creation,

With many a bird's impassioned speeches,

Or a flower's emanation.

O gorgeous Erumango ! isle

Or blossom of the sea !

Often, some long enchanted while,

   Have I been part of thee;

Part of some saffron hue that lingers

   Above thy sapphire mountains;

. One of thy spice-groves' full-voiced singers;

   One of thy murmuring fountains.

And having lived all lives of thine

   That blend with flower or palm,

Or soar in light or soft recline

   In depths of shade and calm;

Once more my soul hath gone forth, flying

   On wings of rich emotion,

· To emerald fair Emoa, lying

   Green on the azure ocean.

     *   *   *

But I, whose freed soul voyages far,

   Do pass my working day

'Mid hardened lives, where no dreams are,
   In straitened speech and way :
Therefore that bark, O shipmen, stay not,
   But let it sail securely,
For—ceased *that* voyaging—I, who may not,
   Should die or go mad surely.

ZULEIKA.

ZULEIKA is fled away,
 Though your bolts and your bars were
  strong;
A minstrel came to the gate to-day
 And stole her away with a song.
His song was subtle and sweet,
It made her young heart beat,
 It gave a thrill to her faint heart's will,
And wings to her weary feet.

Zuleika was not for ye,
 Though your laws and your threats were hard;
The minstrel came from beyond the sea,
 And took her in spite of your guard :

His ladder of song was slight,
But it reached to her window height;
   Each verse so frail was the silken rail
From which her soul took flight.

The minstrel was fair and young;
   His heart was of love and fire;
His song was such as you ne'er have sung,
   And only love could inspire:
He sang of the singing trees,
And the passionate sighing seas,
   And the lovely land of his minstrel band;
And with many a song like these

He drew her forth to the distant wood,
   Where bird and flower were gay,
And in silent joy each green tree stood;
   And with singing along the way,
He drew her to where each bird
Repeated his magic word,

And there seemed a spell she could not tell
In every sound she heard.

And singing and singing still,
　　He lured her away so far,
Past so many a wood and valley and hill,
　　That now, would you know where they are?
In a bark on a silver stream,
As fair as you see in a dream;
　　Lo! the bark glides along to the minstrel's song,
While the smooth waves ripple and gleam.

And soon they will reach the shore
　　Of that land whereof he sings,
And love and song will be evermore
　　The precious, the only things;
They will live and have long delight
They two in each other's sight,
　　In the violet vale of the nightingale,
And the flower that blooms by night.

A SONG OF THE YOUTHS.

L O ! in the palace, lo ! in the street,
    Beautiful beyond measure ;
Yea, gods for glory, and women for sweet,
    The youths, the princes of pleasure !

Idle and crowned in the long day's sun,
    Turbulent, passionate, sad ;
Full of the soul of the deed to be done,
    Or the thought of the joy latest had ;
They walk their way through the crowds that run,
    They pass through the crowds that part ;
And the women behold them, and each knows one,
    How mighty he is in her heart.

Lo ! in the palace, lo ! in the street,
  Beautiful beyond measure ;
Yea, gods for glory, and women for sweet,
  The youths, the princes of pleasure !

They win with the vehemence of their souls,
  With the swiftness of their fame ;
Their strong and radiant look controls,
  And smiles the world to shame.
Their rule is large, and like fair lords,
  They lavish a goodly treasure ;
They live of the joy the world affords,
  And they pay the world with pleasure.

One passes bright through the street down there,
  Named and known of repute ;
And one hath a scandal of rich flowing hair,
  And the musical tongue of a lute.
O the women, beholding, who thrill and say,
  " While that one stays on the earth,

I can have in the secret of night or of day,

    More delight than a man's life is worth !"

O the woman that says in the midst of the crowd,

    " Beautiful, turbulent one,

Do I not know you through semblance and shroud,

    Even as I know the sun ?

Burning, and swift, and divine you are ;

    But I have you all to treasure ;

Women may love you, but mine you are,

    And prince of the princes of pleasure."

Lo ! in the palace, lo ! in the street,

    Beautiful beyond measure ;

Yea, gods for glory, and women for sweet,

    The youths, the princes of pleasure !

SUPREME SUMMER.

O HEART full of song in the sweet song-weather,
    A voice fills each bower, a wing shakes each
      tree,
Come forth, O winged singer, on song's fairest feather,
    And make a sweet fame of my love and of me.

The blithe world shall ever have fair loving leisure,
    And long is the summer for bird and for bee ;
But too short the summer and too keen the pleasure
    Of me kissing her and of her kissing me.

Songs shall not cease of the hills and the heather ;
    Songs shall not fail of the land and the sea :

But, O heart, if you sing not while we·are together,
What man shall remember my love or me?

Some million of summers hath been and not known
    her,
    Hath known and forgotten loves less fair than she;
But one summer knew her, and grew glad to own
    her,
    And made her its flower, and gave her to me.

And she and I, loving, on earth seem to sever
    Some part of the great blue from heaven each
    day:
I know that the heaven and the earth are for ever,
    But that which we take shall with us pass away.

And that which she gives me shall be for no lover
    In any new love-time, the world's lasting while;
The world, when it loses, shall never recover
    The gold of her hair nor the sun of her smile.

A tree grows in heaven, where no season blanches

　Or stays the new fruit through the long golden

　　clime ;

My love reaches up, takes a fruit from its branches,

　And gives it to me to be mine for all time.

What care I for other fruits, fed with new fire,

　Plucked down by new lovers in fair future line ?

The fruit that I have is the thing I desire,

　To live of and die of—the sweet she makes mine.

And she and I, loving, are king of one summer

　And queen of one summer to gather and glean :

The world is for us what no fair future comer

　Shall find it or dream it could ever have been.

The earth, as we lie on its bosom, seems pressing

　A heart up to bear us and mix with our heart;

The blue, as we wonder, drops down a great blessing

　That soothes us and fills us and makes the tears

　　start.

The summer is full of strange hundredth-year flowers,

    That breathe all their lives the warm .air of our

        love,

And never shall know a love other than ours

    Till once more some phœnix-star flowers above.

The silver cloud passing is friend of our loving ;

    The sea, never knowing this year from last year,

Is thick with fair words, between roaring and sough-

        ing,

    For her and me only to gather and hear.

Yea, the life that we lead now is better and sweeter,

    I think, than shall be in the world by and bye ;

For those days, be they longer or fewer or fleeter,

    I will not exchange on the day that I die.

I shall die when the rose-tree about and above me

    Her red kissing mouth seems hath kissed summer

        through :

I shall die on the day that she ceases to love me—

But that will not be till the day she dies too.

Then, fall on us, dead leaves of our dear roses,

And, ruins of summer, fall on us ere long,

And hide us away where our dead year reposes ;

Let all that we leave in the world be—a song.

And, O song that I sing now while we are together,

Go, sing to some new year of women and men,

How I and she loved in the long loving weather,

And ask if they love on as we two loved then.

SONG.

Now I am on the earth,
  What sweet things love me?
Summer, that gave me birth,
  And glows on still above me;
The bird I loved a little while;
  The rose I planted;
The woman in whose golden smile
  Life seems enchanted.

Now I am in the grave,
  What sweet things mourn me?
Summer, that all joys gave,
  Whence death, alas! hath torn me;

One bird that sang to me ; one rose

Whose beauty moved me ;

One changeless woman ; yea, all those

That living loved me.

ANDALUSIAN MOONLIGHT.

IN a lifted palace I dwell apart,
    Changeful in glimmer and shade ;
Alone with my dream, and alone with my heart,
    And the music my life hath made.
      There, deep in the dimness,
      Some white pillar's slimness
Figures my dreamlike thought ;
      And, fainting in flowers,
      Some fountain for hours
Murmurs over my music untaught.

When midnight renders the place more fair
    With shadowy magic and thrill,

And the moonlight floods all the odorous air,

Beneath on the rustling hill;

I see red roses

In the laurel closes,

And the glossy citron-trees;

And thought re-fashions

Past life and passions,

As the moonlight glorifies these.

THE DISEASE OF THE SOUL.

O EXQUISITE malady of the Soul,
   How hast thou marred me !

Once I was goodly and whole—
   Is it a tale or a dream ?—
Sitting where great rivers roll,
   Ruling where great cities gleam,
Full of the sun and the sea,
Fearless and shameless and free,
Queen, for no man to control,
   Woman, for all men to regard me.

O mystical malady of the Soul,
How hast thou marred me !

Lovely the dawn grew upon me,
Golden the day came before me ;
There was no queen that outshone me,
There was no king that withstood—
Come from his East to adore me,
Crowns were the gifts that he bore me,
Quitting his throne to enthrone me,
Queen of supreme womanhood.

Mine were the odorous bowers
On Tiber river and Nile ;
The orgies of fabulous hours,
Under the spell of a smile ;
Greek houses and Orient towers ;
Euphrates' glittering mile ;
And galleys agleam with flowers,
That float to the amorous isle.

All lands had taken my beauty
   For song to the lute and the lyre;
And I had taken for duty
   To live for a song to the lands—
A song of love and desire—
A song of costly attire,
Of gifts and the curious booty
   That strange kings left in my hands.

Born the world's sweetest wonder,
   I came from nearer the sun;
From Babylon then with the plunder,
   Ere Rome's great reign was begun;
Then, O the blithe skies I lived under,
   The gold and the glory I won—
Till my South was broken asunder,
   And out of the North came the Hun!

My face was kissed by the morning,
   My body was kissed all night,

The women kissed me, adorning

My beautiful limbs for the bath

I stood forth, and knew that the sight

Of my form was the world's delight,

And loving and laughing and scorning,

I passed down the day's fair path.

Nothing concealed me or checked me,

While none could bring me to shame ;

The purple, the saffron robe decked me,

But I shone through like a flame.

No evil or sorrow had wrecked me,

No sin had lent me its name ;

What need might there be to protect me,

Where all men loved me the same ?

My love was rich as the ocean

With buried spoil-ships teeming,

Deep-hued and with wonderful motion,

And singing by night and day ;

No space was given to dreaming,

All love was so goodly seeming,

And life was one long emotion,

    That knew nor loss nor delay.

I moved in the market fearless,

    I walked down the joyous street;

I stood in the palace peerless,

    I was so fair and so sweet.

Of many a thing I was careless,

    For all things fell at my feet;

And love was lovely and tearless,

    And pleasure with love did meet.

My song is echoed and ended,

    And where are they gone, my lovers?

My picture is faded and blended

    With the dust of palace and tomb.

The hermit only discovers

The shape that delighted my lovers;

And a shadow of hair still splendid
  And luminous in the gloom.
As ruined and ravished and slain,
  In the day of the ruin of Rome,
I fell with the dead, and have lain
  Long years in the catacomb,
Till my shameless form, without stain,
  And bare and fair as the foam,
Rose a goddess in many a fane,
  Grew a fable in many a home.

But there came to me where I was lying,
  Not death the painless and brief,
But a something stranger than dying,
  That changed me and left me whole—
A malady made of grief
And believing and unbelief,
And of dreaming and hoping and sighing—
  The deathless disease of the Soul.

And I came forth wandering, weeping,
   In a saint's or a mourner's guise,
Like one unrefreshed from sleeping,
   Whom the thoughts and the memories wake,
With the new strange look in my eyes
Of the spirit that never dies,
Of the spirit tormenting and keeping
   The life for the agony's sake.

Oh, the torment of every feeling,
   The sorrow of every smile ;
The smile of my life concealing
   The pain of my heart within !
Oh, the love that my thoughts revile,
With memory there all the while ;
And the ruinous shame revealing
   The secret ruin of sin !

My red mouth fashioned for joy,
   Rich bloom of the world's fairest hour,

Is pale with faint kisses that cloy
And sadden and wither and sting;
My form, like a blue-veined flower,
Has learned to droop and to cower;
And my loves are griefs that destroy
The lovers to whom I cling.

I have seen all heaven in a vision
That life hath clouded and hidden;
I am blinded and deaf with collision
Of lights and clangour of chimes.
And surely my spirit is chidden,
Lifelong for the brief joy forbidden,
The rapture unearthly, Elysian,
That lifts me to heaven at times.

There are infinite sources of tears
Down there in my infinite heart,
Where the record of time appears
As the record of love's deceiving;

Farewells and words that part

Are ever ready to start

To my lips, turned white with the fears

Of my heart, turned sick of believing.

I have dreamed in the red sun-setting,

Among rocks where the sea comes and goes,

Vast dreams of the soul's begetting,

Vague oceans that break on no shore ;

I have felt the eternal woes

Of the soul that aspires and knows ;

Henceforth there can be no forgetting,

Or closing the eyes any more.

From the night's lone meditation,

From the thought in the glowing noon,

I have gathered the revelation,

And all is suffered and known—

I have felt the unearthly swoon

Of the sadness of the moon—

H

I have had of the whole creation
   The secret that makes it groan.

I have put my ear to the earth,
   And heard in a little space
The lonely travail of birth,
   And the lonely prayer of the dying;
I have looked all heaven in the face,
And sought for a holier place,
And a love of my own love's worth,
   And the Soul is the only replying.

I have dwelt in the tomb's drear hollow,
   I have plundered and wearied death,
Till no poison is left me to swallow,
   No dull, sweet Lethe to have.
I have heard all things that he saith,
I have mingled my breath with his breath;
And the phantom of life that I follow
   Is weary with seeking a grave.

It hath led me to terrible places,

Dim oceans and dreadful abysses,

And solitudes teeming with faces

As fair and as wan as my own ;

I have followed the lure of strange blisses,

And fallen asleep under kisses,

To awake in the comfortless spaces

Of desolate dreams of my own.

I know all men, and read in their eyes

A death and a sentence of days ;

I exchange magic words and replies

With the phantoms and fates hanging o'er them:

And my lovers have wearisome ways,

For I know all their love and their praise,

And they echo the words and the sighs

That were echoes of others before them.

They deceive me not, or they deceive me—

'Tis nothing to heaven or hell ;

I charm them, and make them believe me,
    I promise and do not give ;
With hope and despair I dwell,
Between farewell and farewell ;
And my life is the same when they leave me—
    My life that I do not live ;—

            .

My life of the infinite aching,
    My thought of the passionate theme,
My heart that is secretly breaking
    For more than each lover can guess ;
With all these I but suffer or seem ;
But I live in the life that I dream,
With a sorrowful love of my making,
    And a lover I do not possess.

And a part of me still abides
    In ruinous castles remote,
With the sound of disconsolate tides,
    And the echo of desolate mountains ;

They are mine the sighs that float

On the dismal waves of the moat,

And I am the ghost that glides

    Through the paths by the broken fountains.

As queen, then, or lady peerless,

    Or siren cruel and cold,

Or captive forgotten and cheerless,

    I lived, or suffered, or slept ;

So that ages and lives untold

Have left me weary and old ;

I am joyless with joy, and tearless

    With all the tears I have wept.

The nostalgies of dim pasts seize me ;

    There are days when the thought of some Pharaoh

Like a phantom pursues me or flees me

    Through dim lapses of life I forget;

When the love of some fabulous hero,

Or the passion of purple Nero,

Is the one human love that could please me,
    The thing I dream or regret.

There are nights when I live in the azure,
    The life of an angel or star,
When my thought may soar to and measure
    The sky of its hopeless ideal,
And the future, however far,
Seems better than all things that are,
With its wonderful promise of pleasure,
    However strange and unreal.

My wide eyes, weary with seeing,   .
    Are soothed in the twilight of time,
And the formless passion of being,
    Grown wordless with speech profound,
Is sent forth in the mystical clime
Of music celestial, sublime,
Where new unknown spirits are freeing
    Sonorous creations of sound.

And the sun hath long faded away,

And the frank fair world of the light,

With the jubilant life of the day

Become joyless and spectral and hollow ;

But my eyes are seeking for sight,

In the inward and endless night,

Where my lips are learning to pray

To the dreams and the shadows I follow.

And I would that the world were over,

And I, with no dull earth clinging,

Might break through some death and discover

The mystical heaven that nears ;

For it seems that my ears are ringing

With a seraph's beautiful singing,

And the song of no human lover

Can move me again to tears.

O fantasy monstrous, sublime !

O Soul, thou most exquisite madness !

The disease of my life and my time ;
  Corrupt flower of the heart's decay,
Have I bartered my perfect gladness
For an unknown immortal sadness ?
Have I counted my pleasure a crime,
  And wept all my beauty away ?

Yea, for these are too surely thy traces,
  O malady secret and strange !
The frail hues and the cheeks' wan places,
  The eloquent tombs of the tears ;
The uplifted looks that estrange,
And many a mystical change,
And subtle and sorrowful graces,
  The beauty of sorrowful years.

My face keeps the pallid reflection
  Of ecstasies subtle and rare,
The high joy or the sombre dejection
  That comes of unearthly bliss ;

Its wan sad oval is fair

With each fallen angel's despair,

And my lips have the languid complexion

Of the phantom loves that they kiss.

A DREAM.

A DREAM took hold of the heart of a man,
   To hold it more than a mere dream can ;
For the dream was wonderful, glorious, bright,
A splendour by day and a love by night,
In an earth all heaven, in a heaven all light—
For the dream was a woman, womanly, white.

And the dream became such a part of the man,
That it did for him more than a mere dream can ;
For soothing sorrows, transforming tears,
It lifted him higher than hopes and fears ;
It dwelt with him days, and months, and years,
Made love and religion, and faith and prayers.

And who need be told how that dream began

To fail and to fade from the heart of the man ;

Nay, it vanished, it broke, as the fitfullest gleam

Of the sun that fades on the fitfullest stream ;

And there went with it love and religion, I deem,

And faith, and glory, and hope, it would seem ;

For that dream was a woman, that woman a dream.

A SONG OF THE HOLY SPIRIT.

THE Holy Spirit left a habitation
    On the dim shore of heaven's eternal sea,
And named in no man's prayer or invocation,
    Unknown and unbelieved in, save by me ;—
The Holy Spirit looked down through creation
    Upon the things that are and that shall be.

He saw the things that evermore were holy
    Over the wide and many-peopled earth ;
He saw the great proud folk, he saw the lowly,
    The glory and the sadness and the mirth ;
And gazing on them all, he gathered slowly
    The worthlessness within them or the worth.

And lo ! the things whose irrepressible fairness,

    Rebuked by man, lay grieving, now they burst,

All tear-stained, out of darkness into clearness,

    And stood forth beautiful as at the first ;

Feeling indeed the Holy Spirit's nearness ;

    Indeed forgetting man had called them curst.

For unto them a momentary wonder

    Seemed passing in the world : the long hushed eve

Glowed purple, and the awed soul of the thunder

    Lay shuddering in the distance ; and the heave

Of great unsolaced seas over and under

    The tremulous earth was heard with them to

    grieve.

And all they—loves and lovers whose fair faces

    Were piteous in the passion and the shame

Of loving—men and women of all races,

    Together with the great sad voice that came

Out of the sea, and from the earth's deep places,
    They called upon the God who hath no name.

They could not turn away into the sadness;
    They yearned up to the heaven's eternal blue;
And the soul's sobbing almost rose to madness
    Within them, as they longed indeed, and knew
The other folk in holiness and gladness,
    And they might not be glad and holy too.

Alas! all shameful as they were, and chidden,
    They could not quite forsake, nor all forget,
Pure birthrights confiscated and forbidden,
    And heaven itself they loved a little yet;
They would creep in to weep and lie there hidden
    In some dim region where the sun had set.

For many a time some glorified emotion,
    Celestial sister of earth's holiest grief,

Would roll into their hearts like a rich ocean,

Mysterious sympathies that brought belief,

And the heart, flowering upward in devotion,

Cast off the earthly sorrow like a leaf.

And the immense sweet passion, sole oppressing

The unrequited lives it famished in,

Would bear an angel's part of some wide blessing

Shed splendidly above the stars, or win

Pure resignations richer than possessing,

And feel indeed full little like a sin.

A thousand wild-eyed women, fallen or daunted

Before the world's hard hate or insolent smile,

Afraid to look upon the beauty vaunted

And loved, then curst and outlawed, and made
vile,

Wept in the night, or with drooped faces haunted

Drear moaning lakes and many a distant isle.

A thousand faultless-formed ones, made for linking
    Angelic races of the earth and star,
Lay with unprized and priceless splendour shrinking
    Into the shadows of the darkness, far,
Ay, far from love; their lamentable thinking
    Tempting them down to where lost Edens are.

And wandering abroad through every nation
    Were glorious pairs of lovers, whose delight
Some priest had branded with abomination;
    Who went on loving through short day and night,
Homeless and driven from their generation,
    Dying without a name and out of sight.

And all the passionate poets had for glory
    Their exile, and a scandal for their theme;
And only fond faith in an ancient story,
    And heart's allegiance to their heart's fair dream.
Cold youth and impotence, grown old and hoary,
    Hurried men deathward on a frozen stream.

Yea, and that radiant One, the world's immortal,

Unchanging soul and self of the true earth,

Was now a wanderer, grieving like a mortal,

Dishonoured in his grieving and his dearth,

Sitting disconsolate beneath the portal

Of pampered idols served with hollow mirth ;

Yea, the great inward Love, secretly burning

In the deep silent hearts that never spoke,

But shrouded up the passion of their yearning—

Yea, he was king indeed of a sad folk,

Weary wellnigh past hope of his returning,

Sinking wellnigh beneath a joyless yoke.

And only in rare lapses, something dimmer

Than wonted summer eves, when strange stars

trode

The air with mystic steps, that left a shimmer

And shook down perfume on the awakened sod,

I

Dared they look up and soothe them with the glimmer

Of distant heaven, or think at all of God—

And then there was no hope they might inherit,

No way with any god whose way was known;

Their passionate souls within them had no merit,

Only the piteous passion there alone;

And then—but on that night the Holy Spirit

Saw them and loved and saved them for His own.

He opened like a bosom the great heaven;

He dropped a silver whisper through the air,

And in all desolate lands where they were driven

He reached, and wrought a blessing on them there;

And the great sins they had are all forgiven,

And their great love is only great and fair.

He looked upon them all, and wide compassion

He felt for all their exile and their dole;

He gave a holy name to their deep passion,

And made a new religion for their soul ;

For they were perfected in God's own fashion,

To be a part of God's ineffable whole.

He gazed through all the impious shrouds enfold-
ing,

With dire disfigurement of lust and fear,

The splendid beauty of each woman's moulding

That his creating kiss had left so dear :

The Holy Spirit marvelled in beholding

How it was lost and held accursed down here.

And once more, mightily and most securely,

That desecrated loveliness shall shine,

And the sweet poet passionately and purely

May worship it in his heart's fairest shrine,

For O the Holy Spirit blessed it surely,

And said it was for ever most divine.

And henceforth, O ye hard folk who go steeling
  Your lives against all love with lust and pride,
Know that full many a whole and mystic heal-
    ing
  Is come into the heart that else had died ;
And many a piteous outcast human feeling
  A kinder God than yours hath sanctified.

That night I did behold the great blue dwelling
  Through which the soul goes upward; and the
    dome
Of its ineffable height seemed past all telling,
  The perfect heaven, the soul's eternal home !

And I through miracle of love discerning
  The heart of the blue mystery above,
I prayed a few words purely with great yearn-
    ing,
  Touching my weak heart and my earthly love.

I said : O Spirit high above all seeming !

   Known by a splendour, seen in a sweet hue,

Reached in the passion of transcendent dreaming,

   Nothing is holy but my heart and You ;

And in my heart laid open for your seeing,

   There is a piteous love, tender and deep,

A love become the deepest part of being—

   I scarce know whether most I sing or weep :

I scarce know whether, sad and lost and human,

   Some earth of hers shall bury me, some hell

Consume me ; only this,—without that woman,

   Heaven were a place wherein I could not dwell ;

The teared-stained place she lies in is my heaven ;

   I took the sin she sinned, till it became

My holiness ; and now I pray not even

   Without some lovely mingling of her name.

Her dear wan life is dearer to me keeping
.   The sear upon its whiteness of her fall ;
The part of me she tarnished with her weeping,
    Let that be saved of me or none at all.

Look down, O Spirit, through the night, distilling
    The blue effusion of a luminous kiss ;
Look into her clear heart, open and thrilling
    Beneath the soaring thoughts whose hidden bliss

Hath long ago exalted above measure
    Of lifelong joy or woe her risen soul,
Risen a spotless sister of the azure
    From a forgotten grave of wrong and dole.

Is she not wonderful, sweet, ay, and holy ?
    Shall she not sit on some transcendent throne ?
Am not I saved in loving her, and solely
    Worthy of heaven in calling her my own ?

—Alas ! then knew I the most infinite distance

    Between that ardent formless One and me ;

My yearning clave far skies with no resistance,

    And felt His emanation like a sea ;

But strange worlds lay between, of dim existence,

    Inward in spiritual mystery.

And through the night's enchanted league still gazing,

    I still beheld the wide ethereal sight

Of all the stars' far palaces amazing

    Moving scintillant in abundant light,

And now and then the lightning went round blazing

    From each to each some message of delight.

Only I heard a mightier prediction,

    A growing and tremendous prophecy,

Feeling the while, with more serene conviction,

    The splendour of the Holy Spirit nigh,

And that in some eternal benediction

    He did include my love and me on high.

Only I saw, as now in evolution

Of season after season, clime on clime,

The azure ocean's gradual revolution,

Sure of the world and of man's heart in time,

And the sweet Holy Spirit's absolution,

Healing, and making each man's love sublime.

GREATER MEMORY.

I N the heart there lay buried for years
   Love's story of passion and tears ;
Of the heaven that two had begun,
  And the horror that tore them apart,
When one was love's slayer, but one
  Made a grave for the love in his heart.

The long years passed weary and lone,
And it lay there and changed there unknown ;
Then one day from its innermost place,
  In the shamed and the ruined love's stead,
Love arose with a glorified face,
  Like an angel that comes from the dead.

It uplifted the stone that was set

On that tomb which the heart held yet;

But the sorrow had mouldered within,

 And there came from the long closed door

A clear image, that was not the sin

 Or the grief that lay buried before.

The grief it was long washed away

In the weeping of many a day;

And the terrible past lay afar,

 Like a dream left behind in the night;

And the memory that woke was a star

 Shining pure in the soul's pure light.

There was never the stain of a tear

On the face that was ever so dear;

'Twas the same in each lovelier way;

 'Twas the old love's holier part,

And the dream of the earliest day

    Brought back to the desolate heart.

It was knowledge of all that had been

In the thought, in the soul unseen ;

'Twas the word which the lips could not say

    To redeem and recover the past ;

It was more than was taken away

    Which the heart got back at the last.

The passion that lost its spell,

The rose that died where it fell,-

The look that was looked in vain,

    The prayer that seemed lost evermore,

They were found in the heart again,

    With all that the heart would restore.

And thenceforward the heart was a shrine

For that memory to dwell in divine,

Till from life, as from love, the dull leaven

Of grief-stained earthliness fell ;

And thenceforth in the infinite heaven

That heart and that memory dwell.

SONG OF A SHRINE.

ONE little unseen snake of memory
    Followed her through the world; and in the
       hour
Of her last desolateness, what foe but he,
    Finding her like a bowed and beaten flower
    Fainting with sadness in a fading bower,
Drew nigh familiar to her, keeping near
    With a sure spell from which she could not start,
Hissed a forgotten farewell in her ear,
    And struck his poignant poison to her heart?

Thither she came by many a gleaming track
    Of wooing light and painless swift forsaking;

Fearless she came, and without looking back,

    And never a lingering word of fond leave-taking ;

    But there at length, alone with her heart breaking,

She only saw dead roses white and red,

And pale leaves' rainy roof-work overhead ;

    She only felt that sting, and knew the aching,

As of a ceaseless worm that gnaws the dead.

Yea, ceaseless—since he had found that day at last,

    Lying in wait for it beneath vain summer,

Tracking it through the transient roses cast

In vain between her and the outraged past

    He came from—ceaseless that insidious comer

Had leave to make his sojourn ; through the world,

    She found some flower to foil him from her breast ;

But flowerless now she lay, and he lay curled,

    Her thought his victim, in her heart his nest.

And all the abortive years were crushed between

    And that day over them reached out a hand

And joined itself to a day dimly seen

Through all years' distance in a distant land.

Inwardly then, with perfect quenchless burning,

The unknown and immeasurable Soul

Opened undying depths of fatal yearning

And unconsoled eternities, all turning

Back to that past's irrevocable goal.

The lovely blossom of that woman's face

Bore fading out in many a tender trace,

Pale flowery legends of love's glowing wonder,

Felt in unfinished flower-time, in some place

Where summer's wing beat rapturously under

Unalterable heaven. But now, alas !

It was as though the earth had leave to plunder

And soulless earth-born things to kiss and pass.

And ruin that fallen flower in the grass.

Oh, I can say that She was once exalted

In the chaste glory of adoring thought,

' Become a temple most serenely vaulted
    With dreamy domes of heaven itself had wrought—
    The wonderful white statue, passion brought,
And set there sacredly to stand and shine—
White sanctity becoming more divine
    In its own fair religion, unassaulted
By doubt, and steadfast as a starry sign.

And the first irremediable sin
And sacrilege that let the day glare in
    On all that glimmering splendour—so appalling
With great rude clash, and bidding death begin
    To drag down what was lifted above falling
Or death,—it was some fatal thought of hers,
The birth of some false dream that grew perverse,
    Even in her plighted heart, and, past recalling,
Lured her and led her to fulfil its curse.

Yea, and how far she went that dreadful way,
    How weary and how long life's murder seemed

To the divine white nature, while it gleamed
With any remnant of a holy ray;
And what things sullied her, I will not say—
Indeed my heart would fail me in the telling—
  Indeed I will not know : let those men keep
  That secret who were there, and saw her weep
In the rent ruin of her heart's last dwelling.

I did not see her then : long years ago
I knew her; but they tell me that she turned
  In that late bitter day, with a great crying
  Torn from her tortured heart, and, like one dying,
With haggard passionate looks she prayed to know
What long-lost way would lead her where she yearned
  To set her foot once more, though but to die;
Where she might look upon the heaven she spurned,
  And him whose love had set her once on high.

Then went she like a woman desolate,
  A burning inward pain feeding her cheek

K

With wavering fire, until she found the strait,
    The stony mountain paths, whose stones could speak
Great deafening memories uncompassionate ;
And onward still, laboriously and slowly,
    She learnt the unrelenting upward road
Out of the world, and, beautiful and holy,
    She saw again the home where he abode.

There was no change : only it rose more clearly
    Into the stainless bosom of the blue ;
Only the pines stood closer, and severely
    The strong ascetic shadow that they threw
    Seemed to have shut upon it ; and she knew
The sombre secret that they seemed to hold
    Eternal converse of from year to year,—
The thing concerning him and her they told
    Loftily there, for only God to hear.

Then did that thousand-headed serpent thing,
    Who had the long existence of her soul.

To plague with ruthless and recurrent sting,

    Urge her to take into her breast the whole

Consummate irremediable hell

    That the last glimpse of a surpassing heaven,

Cut off and vanishing upward, might first tell

    The dismal depth of—loss without a leaven

Of hope, and long remorse profound and fell.

And she drew nigh, in one of her old ways,

    Wherein such snare of sweet used to be set

To fascinate and take the golden rays

    Of his first look in an enchanted net:

She drew nigh ; but she called him not her own

    When she beheld him ;—bitter past believing

    It seemed to her, for he had long ceased grieving,

And day and night he was no more alone ;

But One stood there to heal and to atone.

Through changeless night and day, a changeless face

Sweetened and filled and glorified his place ;

Which the unbroken halos of a dream,

Severed from earth and distanced in their gleam,

Marvellous as a planet's radiant ring :

And never, for the ruin of an hour,

Had come the shadow of a fatal thing

Between the bloom of that celestial flower

And his soul looking up and worshipping.

That vision bore the glory that She had

On lips and hair and white effulgent form ;

That vision kept the love that made her glad,

Blooming up there beyond the rain and storm ;

And an immaculate heart of hers was thrilling

In an unfallen nature without shame,

And realising ever and fulfilling

The perfect heaven of love from which she came,

She who beheld and was no more the same.

And then that other, from the lovely height

Of a surpassing love and spotless white,

Bade her depart and be no longer there—

" I, the sweet stainless splendour that you were ;

I, the unblemished image of your face ;

I, all your virgin and untarnished grace ;

Your soul's sublime betrothal ; your first kiss ;

I have not fallen away from love and bliss ;

Here, in the lifelong wonder of a dream,

I, his soul's sister, crowned with many a gleam

From the clear heights of vision, and still dressed

In tender saffron memories oft caressed,

Have changed not, only that the tears he shed

Have grown to be a halo round my head ;

And unto him, left holier for each tear,

The angel now is dearer than the dear

Exalted woman wept through many a year.

After the night of lamentation long,

After the soul's sad resignation song,

Here, in the cloistral solitudes of grief,

He saw me beautiful, a lost belief,

Restored, transfigured, in some way divine,

" To light up all love's ruins, and to shine

Unshaken on the soul's eternal throne ;

He found again his spotless one, his own,

Sitting beside him, excellent and bright ;

Upon her features there was not the blight

. Of any falseness ; all her passionate gaze

Was bent upon him, mindful of no days

Of sadness and divorce ; and, as before,

He dreamed again a dream that nevermore

Shall leave him.   Oh ! his sorrow is quite past,

Love is so strong and heaven so great at last !

And I, fond image of a faultless love,

Grown winged, immortal with face set above,

And keen illumined look discerning far

All heaven without a break from star to star,

I am that only mistress of his soul,

Dreamed of and waited for and wooed with whole

Transcendency of passion.   Oh ! how fair

That Eden was his first thought did prepare,

With pure unearthly meanings and rare scent

" Of many a speechless delicate intent!

And onward, upward, how the consecrate

White monuments of memory relate

Of many a precious sadness, and the spell

Of faith's celestial flower ineffable,

Grown up miraculously out of all !

And it shall be that not a flower shall fall,

And not a hope shall fail, and not a height

Of love's imagination fond and bright,

Be less than perfected in her, divine—

The pure Ideal of his soul's pure shrine !"

IN LOVE'S ETERNITY.

MY body was part of the sun and the dew,
  Not a trace of my death to me clave,
There was scarce a man left on the earth whom I knew,
  And another was laid in my grave.
I was changed and in heaven, the great sea of blue
  Had long washed my soul pure in its wave.

My sorrow was turned to a beautiful dress,
  Very fair for my weeping was I;
And my heart was renewed, but it bore none the less
  The great wound that had brought me to die,
The deep wound that She gave who wrought all my
    distress;
  Ah, my heart loved her still in the sky!

I wandered alone where the stars' tracks were bright ;

I was beauteous and holy and sad ;

I was thinking of her who of old had the might

To have blest me, and made my death glad ;

I remembered how faithless she was, and how light,

Yea, and how little pity she had.

The love that I bore her was now more sublime ;

It would never be shared now or known ;

And her wound in my heart was · a pledge in Loves'

clime,

For her sake I was ever alone,

Till the Spirit of God in the fulness of time

Should make perfect all love in His own.

My soul had forgiven each separate tear,

She had bitterly wrung from my eyes ;

But I thought of her lightness,—ah ! sore was my fear

She would fall somewhere never to rise,

And that no one would love her, to bring her soul near

    To the heavens, where love never dies.

She had drawn me with feigning, and held me a day;

    She had taken the passionate price

That my heart gave for love, with no doubt or delay,

    For I thought that her smile would suffice;

She had played with and wasted and then cast away

    The true heart that could never love twice.

And false must she be; she had followed the cheat

    That ends loveless and hopeless below:

I remembered her words' cruel worldly deceit

    When she bade me forget her and go.

She could ne'er have believed after death we might

      meet,

    Or she would not have let me die so.

I thought, and was sad: the blue fathomless seas

    Bore the white clouds in luminous throng;

And the souls that had love were in each one of
    these ;
They passed by with a great upward song :
They were going to wander beneath the fair trees,
    In high Eden—their joy would be long.

An age it is since : the great passionate bloom
    Of eternity burns more intense ;
The whole heaven draws near to its beautiful doom,
    With a deeper, a holier sense ;
It feels ready to fall on His bosom in whom
    Is each love and each love's recompense.

How sweet to look back to that desolate space
    When the heaven scarce my heaven seemed !
She came suddenly, swiftly,—a great healing grace
    Filled her features, and forth from her streamed.
With a cry our lips met, and a long close em-
    brace
    Made the past like a thing I had dreamed.

Ah Love! she began, when I found you were dead,

 I was changed, and the world was changed too ;

On a sudden I felt that the sunshine had fled,

 And the flowers and summer gone too ;

Life but mocked me ; I found there was nothing

  instead,

 But to turn back and weep all in you.

When you were not there to fall down at my feet,

 And pour out the whole passionate store

Of the heart that was made to make my heart

  complete,

 In true words that my memory bore,—

Then I found that those words were the only words

  sweet,

 And I knew I should hear them no more.

I found that my life was grown empty again ;

 Day and year now I had but to learn

How my heaven had come to me, sought me in
    vain,
  And was gone from me ne'er to return :
Ah ! too earthly and winterly now seemed the plain
  Of dull life where the heart ceased to burn.

And soon with a gathering halo was seen,
  O'er a dim waste that fell into night,
Your coming, your going, as though it had been
  The fair track of an angel of light ;
And my dream showed you changed in a spirit's full
    sheen,
  Fleeing from me in far lonely flight.

My angel ! 'twas then with a soul's perfect stake
  You came wooing me day after day,
With soft eyes that shed tears for my sake, and the
    sake
  Of intense thoughts your lips would not say.

'Twas a love then like this my heart cared not to
    take !
  'Twas a heart like this I cast away !

Ah, yes ! but your love was a fair magic toy,
    That you gave to a child, who scarce deigned
To glance at it—forsook it for some passing joy,
    Never guessing the charm it contained ;
But you gave it and left it, and none could destroy
    The fair talisman where it remained.

And, surely, no child, but a woman at last
    Found your gift where the child let it lie,
Understood the whole secret it held, sweet and vast,
    The fair treasure a world could not buy ;
And believed not the meaning could ever have past,
    Any more than the giver could die.

And then did that woman's whole life, with a start,
    Own its lover, its saviour, its lord ;

He had come, he had wooed her—and lo! her dull
  heart
  Had not hailed him with one stricken chord
Of whole passion—had suffered him e'en to depart
  Without hope of a lover's reward !

But surely there failed not at length his least look,
  His least pleading, his most secret tear,
To win her and save her; her heart surely took
  A fond record of all : very dear,
Very gracious he seemed ; and for him she forsook
  The drear ruin her soul had come near.

For him she made perfect her life, till she laved
  Her soul pure in the infinite blue :
O thou lover ! who once for a love deathless craved,
  A brief heaven of years frail and few—
Take the child whom you loved, and the woman you
  saved,
  In the angel who now blesses you !

She ceased.   To my soul's deepest sources the sense

   Of her words with a full healing crept,

And my heart was delivered with rapture intense

   From the wound and the void it had kept;

Then I saw that her heart was a heaven immense

   As my love ; and together we wept.

NOSTALGIE DES CIEUX.

HOW far away among the hazy lands
　　That float beneath the rising sun's new rim,
　Ere intervening seas swell to their brim,—
How far away are thy enchanted sands,
Thou half-remembered country, where sweet hands
Anointed me with splendours !　Mystic bands
　　Draw back my dreams to thee, till all grows dim,
　　And in my eyes the tears of yearning swim.

When I was yet a child, it was as though
　　So lately one, I seemed quite to know who
　　Had brought me hither, o'er a space of blue.
My heart remembered perfectly the glow

L

Of wondrous meadows, where strange flowers did
 grow,
That I could pluck a little while ago :
 It was no farther than the birds oft flew,
 I should go back there in a day or two.

I had no need, as now, to close my eyes
 And count the fading memories within ;
 Or in frail dreams seek ever to begin,
And live again an untold past that lies
Behind me now—a legend of fair skies
And dwellings full of light—a paradise,
 So pure, so dazzling, so shut out from sin,
 Sometimes I scarce believe my part therein.

But then I bore, indeed, without a thought,
 Unfinished raptures, fresh from many a place
 Where I had tarried some last moment's space ;
All the rich inward of my soul was fraught

With latest music that my ear had caught

In the far clime that morning; and unsought

  Strange words of joy would flood my lips

    apace,

  And language of swift laughter fill my face.

A thousand thrilling secrets lived in me ;

  Fair things last whispered in that land of mine,

  By those who had most magic to divine

The glowing of its roses, and to see

What burning thoughts they cherished inwardly ;

Yea, and to know the mystic rhapsody

  Of some who sang at a high hidden shrine,

  With voices ringing pure and crystalline. '

And I remembered—yea, as now I dream—

  A goodly company with brows most fair,

  About whose forms, like veils, a shining hair

Fell splendidly and hid them : long the gleam

Of their unfading smile did fondly seem
To play around me in the strange sunbeam
   That gilded the cold place I did compare
   With mine and theirs in that land's balmier
      air.

Ah! soon my heart fell sick with yearning sore,
   E'en toward those, my kinsfolk, and right fain
   I was to see them through the mirage plain
Still looking for me from the well-loved shore;
And soon I thought indeed that he who bore
Me hither should return for me once more:
   But day by day I waited all in vain,
   He never came to take me back again.

Then year by year quite joyless I became,
   For no one understood my words' bright way,
   Till lips and eyes were sealed up with dismay;
And the soul fled from them in grief and shame,

And dwindled to a dulled and hidden flame
Far inward, while there died full many a name
  Within me, and the memories that lay
  At heart gave out a pale and transient ray.

Long time, amazed and dumb, I looked around,
  Seeming a very alien, and alone
  Among a sunless folk I ne'er had known,
Who called themselves my kindred, while they
    bound
My pining spirit with restraints that wound
About its inmost tendrils : Ah ! I found
  It was a desolate land where I was thrown,
  And left too weak to fly back to my own !

They set themselves to maim frail, unfelt wings,
  That used to be the fellows of swift will,
  And bring me softly to each glittering sill
Of joyful palaces, where my heart clings

Now faintly, as in mere fond hoverings,

About a distant dreamwork. Wretched things,

 Cold wraiths of joy, they chained me to, to kill

 My soul, yet rich with many a former thrill.

They set themselves to darken the clear sight,

 Unfailing as a star's, wherewith my glance

 Too surely pierced each semblance like a lance

Of steel; they made me grope with the scarce

  light

Of their own self-deception in their night:

Yea, but for some transcendent dream, there might

 Have grown in me a balm of tolerance,

 And I found joy among their joys perchance!

I have learned through their sad and sickly lore

 Of heart and brain—yea, since I was not free,

 I have with perfect feigning bowed the knee,

And framed my lips in set words to implore

Such meeds of seeming bliss as their lives store

To crown them with—yea, since their language bore

  No word at all for aught of what might be

  Content of one desire conceived by me.

But I am weak among them, cannot seem

  Full-hearted in their life ; with many a look

  I wound them or repel ; they cannot brook

My coldness : Ah ! their chill sun hath no beam

To cure my foreign fairness, and a gleam

Of Edens lost, scarce better than a dream,

  Was on me when their boasted prize I took,

  Unflushed, as though I gained not, but forsook !

I hate their grave profanity, that drapes

  With royal right of sanctified intent

  Base greeds in which their common lives are

    spent

With honoured name ; I loathe the lust that apes

A passion, and in coarse fruition shapes
No flower of fair regret, but straight escapes
   From all the richer joy and sorrow blent
   In after-thinking, as from punishment.

I hate the heavy sham of wits, that find,
   Examine, lose, and refind that sole grain
   Of rarest gold-dust on a golden plain,
Their science—leaving thousand-fold behind
Mysterious tracts of knowledge, that my mind
Scans with some inner vision not yet blind,
   Like flash of memory striving to regain
   Possession of a heart's once bright domain.

Yea, with their dreary creeds, their life's pale
      bloom,
   Their science, all of matter, that just plays
   With the external slough as it decays
Left by some risen spirit near his tomb,—

They seem indeed to dwell in lower gloom
Of mansions, through whose every upper room,
  Made wonderful with full and cloudless rays,
  My winged soul passed in splendid former days.

But ofttimes—when, perhaps, beneath the glare
  Of one of their coarse tinselled shows, I sit
  Lone in their midst—in spite of some fond fit
Of self-sufficing thoughts, with piteous stare,
Their upturned faces seeking to stay care,
And fire lives.soulless, dreamless, with those bare,
  Most tawdry splendours their own hands have
    lit—
  Plead to my heart and sorely trouble it.

And I am on a sudden changed, and filled
  With an immense compassion, with a deep,
  Almighty yearning to those men who reap
No real good all their days, who ne'er have thrilled

With one rich touch of joy, whose lives creep
    chilled
From sunless childhoods with dull pulses stilled
    In dreamless deaths ; their souls no memory keep,
    And in their lives are no fair pasts to weep.

Oh, then my heart within feels nigh to break
    With vast desire to soothe some perfect way
    Those joyless men ; to lend their languid day
A gleam of hope, their night, some trance to make
The deathly darkness holier : for their sake
Tears flood my eyes, and worlds of pity ache
    About slow sources of cold speech and stay
    For one great word my lips ne'er find to say.

I long—yea, for a space—to draw more near,
    And join my comfort with their hearts' dull mood ;
    I burn to tell in their own tongue the good
I mean to them, the pity my thoughts bear :

Alas ! I could not speak, they could not hear,

No dream of mine to their eyes could appear ;

  Vain, the thoughts go back to the heart to brood,

  Ere I have spoken or they understood.

FROM HEAVEN TO HELL.

QUITE long ago there was a day
    (A picture wellnigh washed away
Its memory seems), when, as though One
Preparing some new world with sun
And flowers for me, having quite done,
Touched my heart keenly, bade it break
And bloom for summer's sake,—
I seemed in sudden summer to awake.

Beside me the first woman stood,
    And looked on me for the first time.
Between the pathway and the wood
    She seemed to make a softer clime

For vervein, violet, and thyme :
I saw her as she seemed ; but she,
Seeing herself and me,
Knew the last day there with the first, maybe.

A great flood forced my lips to part
And speak the heart's word.   O my heart !
    That felt scarce holy in the fair
    New earth, for so her beauty there
    Seemed to be hallowing earth and air,
Changing the world some unknown way—
Alas ! for on that day
My heart was even holier than all they !

Its one word filled up all the space
Between me praying and the place
    I thought God dwelt in ; sure the blue
    Would know and let the answer through,
    And her lips would but speak it too ;
And when my heart went forth to say—

Is she not mine alway?

Lo ! heaven and earth and her own lips said, Yea.

My innermost and farthest life

Came to her, made her more than wife ;

   And I can say that every thought

   Went to eternity, and sought

   The safe place where we should be brought—

I leading her, as she first led

Me by that word she said—

The heaven I loved for, who have hell instead.

'Twas she who marred it all, not I ;

'Twas she who left me there to die,

   Fallen, and calling on her still.

   Her own heart called her to fulfil

   Some hundredth plight with her own ill.

From my hell here I cannot see

How far her hell may be ;—

And yet there was a heaven for her and me !

Then in that dark, while some torn shred

Of the great lights extinguishèd

Writhed on and flickered o'er my head,

The second woman found me fair,

With fading crowns still on my hair,

And, through the nights I could not bear,

The second woman said—

" There is another heaven in that one's stead."

A new earth seemed she, and her mouth

Some hotter summer of the south ;

And, when she too murmured *"Alway,"*

The word still seemed to reach and stay

In some far blue ; and I can say

Long time beside her did I lie,

Hoping to see by and by

Some silver vista of eternity.

\

Only, at length, beholding long

Her lurid beauty, in the strong

Red radiance of my burning soul,

I knew how terrible and whole

A ruin drew me from the goal

I dreamed of; then my heart I bent

To love what her love meant.

She left me, and I know not where she went.

And, after that, the herd and swarm

Of the wild beasts in woman's form

That make the fallen heart their prey,

And tear it part from part, and slay

The remnant of it day by day,

Came round about me.   In the gloom

Between me and the tomb,

I neither hope, nor grieve : I wait for doom.

These lynxes find me in the lone

Foul sepulchre where I am thrown ;

Upon their yellow dappled hair

My last light dies ; but some long glare

Of endless hell comes straight and bare

Out of their eyes.   And these have done

Their fierce will one by one ;

So I am what I am, and what you shun.

TO A YOUNG MURDERESS.

FAIR yellow murderess, whose gilded head
    Gleaming with deaths; whose deadly body
      white,
Writ o'er with secret records of the dead;
    Whose tranquil eyes, that hide the dead from sight
Down in their tenderest depth and bluest bloom;
    Whose strange unnatural grace, whose prolonged
      youth,
Are for my death now and the shameful doom
    Of all the man I might have been in truth,

Your fell smile, sweetened still, lest I might shun
    Its lingering murder, with a kiss for lure,

Is like the fascinating steel that one
  Most vengeful in his last revenge, and sure
The victim lies beneath him, passes slow,
  Again and oft again before his eyes,
And over all his frame, that he may know
  And suffer the whole death before he dies.

Will you not slay me? Stab me; yea, somehow,
  Deep in the heart : say some foul word to last,
And let me hate you as I love you now.
  Oh, would I might but see you turn and cast
That false fair beauty that you e'en shall lose,
  And fall down there and writhe about my feet,
The crooked loathly viper I shall bruise
  Through all eternity :—

                    Nay, kiss me, Sweet!

SUCH as I am become, I walked one day
    Along a sombre and descending way,
Not boldly, but with dull and desperate thought :
Then one who seemed an angel—for 'twas He,
My old aspiring self, no longer *Me*—
Came up against me terrible, and sought
To slay me with the dread I had to see
His sinless and exalted brow.   We fought ;
And, full of hate, he smote me, saying, " Thee
I curse this hour : go downward to thine hell."
And in that hour I felt his curse and fell.

AT THE LAST.

BY weary paths and wide
  Up many a torn hillside,
Through all the raging strife
And the wandering of life,
Here on the mountain's brow
I find, I know not how,
My long-neglected shrine
Still holy, still mine.

The wall, with leaves o'ergrown,
Is ruined but not o'erthrown ;
Surely the door hath been
Guarded by one unseen ;

Surely the prayer last prayed

And the dream last dreamed have stayed.

I will enter, and try once more

To dream and pray as of yore.

I T is no longer the aching, inconsolable thought
of my lost love—of her who was made to be
mine, who was mine, and shall never be mine
again, while I live desiring her,—that fills me
at this moment ;

It is not the thought of the pale passionless semblance of a love I have tried to put in the place
thereof;

It is no tardy ambition to arise even now out of grief,
and become such as I might have been,—

Great even in spite of grief, greater perhaps because
of grief.

Neither is it even grief!

It is just a strange, quiet thought, scarcely sweet,
scarcely sad, of the Earth out of which I came,
and into which I shall once more return.

The day has been hot, lagging, and weary; no pleasure
in sun or shade—no flower's scent all day long.

Now the faint distant thunders have worked a soft
change in the air, and set free cool many-coloured
clouds wandering about the sky;

And a few great drops of rain have splashed upon
leaves, and trickled down here and there, some
into dry open mouths of flowers, some into the
close July dust.

Very bitter and full of anguish has the day seemed to
my heart through the long weary hours, till the
evening came, and I wept.

And now everything has wept : there are many flower
scents abroad in the air, heavy and fitful; but
the separate scent that comes up from the cool,
damp Earth gets nearest to my heart :
The dull, unalterable emanation of the unseen Earth
down there is all that my heart takes note of :
Yes; and I have ceased weeping.

It is wonderful that I never preferred the thought of
you before, O still, mysterious, unalterable Earth !
It is wonderful that I never longed to know you, to
feel you, to become one with you ; that I never
. had strange revelations of you in dreams ; that I
never stopped loving, or thinking, or speaking, or
singing, to consider about and understand you :
It is most wonderful that I never stopped suffering,
to think how undisturbed, and changeless, and
full of rest is the Earth out of which I came, and
to which I shall one day return.

For these others—the world of men and women, the world of beasts and of birds, of flowers and leaves, summer, winter,—the very air, and the clouds, and the sky, are full of the trouble and bitterness of change, as I am :

They are all agitated as I am :

They all suffer.

I hear some one weeping wherever I go, and a bird chanting dolefully in every green place :

But you are so like the ineffable, unattainable thing I have always desired to become—quite peaceful, eternal ; never suffering, perhaps never feeling.

O kind maternal Earth !

Keep the unborn in your bosom—keep it ever in your bosom unborn :

Keep the seeds, and the bulbs, and the roots, and the whole new world, your child, in your bosom ever unborn.

The heart within me has never once known rest.

You have remained in the happiest repose, made glad
    by every lily and cowslip and common heartsease
    and blade of grass that has grown for a thousand
    years ;
And I have lived all my life in such a very few years,
    and am not made happy by one thing that I
    have done or lived for.

I have only lived for one thing :
With as great a love as you, O mother Earth, have
    given to the whole of your lilies and grasses, and
    all your creatures for a thousand years, I have
    loved that one creature whom I have lived for.
One day when she was all mine, and our two hearts
    felt and knew everything at the same moment,
    the sky being more superbly blue than I had ever
    known it before, or have since beheld it, I saw

a wonderful hand in the midst of the blue, writing—Eternity.

I felt sure she saw it too, and that the same thought
    came into her heart as into mine just then.

(Alas! I have learned since that too many of my very
    best feelings were never shared by her, or known
    at all to her.)
From that time I have striven to keep her mine; I
    have striven with every moment and hour and
    day, as a man strives with every wave to reach
    the opposite shore of a river;
I have wrestled for her with the whole of hell,
And with herself:
I have fought for her with every creature on the face
    of the globe.

And such a small part of eternity is over yet!

But my whole strength is already used up, and she is
still living.

O mother! I feel a great desire to tell you all this.

See how foolish and agitated and frantic I have been,
and how I have suffered. I think if I were to
be quite with you now, I should have enough to
tell you for ever.

You must teach me to bear this, as you bear the loss
of so mahy lilies and other flowers for so many
thousand years.

And, indeed, if you are such as you seem to me now,
how could you ever give birth to one such as I
am?

Down there, under the blades of grass, under the
leaves, under the tiny flowers, under the great
trees, are soft shy sounds of trickling rain, or dew
melting, or wind blowing, or things stirring and
rustling; such sounds as you might hear through

your sleep without waking or being troubled: but there is never a sound of any sighing, or weeping, or complaining down there so near to the quiet Earth.

At this moment the world is nothing to me, the summer is nothing to me, nor the scented air, nor the greenest, happiest place : I have neither sister nor brother nor friend nor lover; I have only my mother, the cold brown Earth.

I used to believe that my father, who left me here a long while ago, was still living far away somewhere in the remote splendid immensity of the blue : I was not sure that the blue was not indeed some part of him. I used to think I should become greater in every sense, till I found out where he was or reached him, or it became necessary for me to be taken wherever he might be.

But just now it seems I am too weak for all that; it

seems I would rather lie down and sleep for a long time, and forget all that has ever happened to me, and perhaps never wake again.

Since I have suffered, no place seems fitter for me than the bosom of my mother, the still, the cold, the unalterable Earth.

ODE TO A NEW AGE.

H AIL! for long thoughts have hailed thee in our
     hearts—

Age, that art glorious—Age, that art all golden,

Hail! for at length out of fair distance starts

The dawn of thy sweet presence, long withholden,

Murmurous, as with some new sound that parts

Pale lips, moved with some inward new emotion;

As with faint stirs of chill breath breaking sleep,

Or tremulous delight of brooding wings,

That cover a pure place serene and deep,

Where there is glow, and strange and mingled motion

Of lights, and births of many golden things.

For all we wait tormented with great needs ;

And having served a long expectancy,

Yea, having laboured, yea, having sown seeds,

And knowing not what sort of thing should be

Of that we sowed, whether a thing for good,

A crown as of pure wheat, begetting mirth

And blessing at the last, or some false bloom,

Mere chaff and husk, which shall not have withstood

A wind ere falling fruitless to the earth,—

We hail and welcome with full faith the doom,

Knowing not yet what God shall give us love,

Calling on many gods ; but all for thee,

Great Age, we hasten : be thou soon above,

An all-sufficing firmament, a sun

Fit for the worship of these souls that see

With no false sight, nor faithlessly in dreams,

Thee present, feeling, as it were, some gleams

Fore-haloed, some sweet breath that doth fore-run

The full fertility that thou shalt breathe

At last upon them waking.   For we are pushed

N

So forward by these blind thoughts in our hearts,

As first, when we were in the dark beneath,

No holier than all weak and hidden parts

Of weeds or flowers, we were so blindly pushed

Towards life, with sudden and new conscious need

Of light, when love as yet we knew not—even

As hitherto we have been urged and driven

With foremost hearts : yea, we are moved indeed,

And troubled waiting.   Full of care, we cry,

Who is this God—and these He giveth birth,

Having enkindled them with some new spark

Out of unmoulded essences, that lie   ·

In soft cores and recesses of the earth,

Or rot in realms of the limitless dark,

Unwarmed and unawakened?   Yea, what worth

Of love is here that we should barter sleep?

To lack love, waking, and live doubtful years,

Knowing not whether most to laugh or weep,

Feeding our souls on hoping, and our ears

Too fain with any music that deceives,

With moaning voice of winds or ocean sigh,

Or insufficient lisping of the leaves?

To feel some little light, and hear a cry

And live, and see no miracle and die?

Nay, by yon pink of slowly parting lips,

A long rim near the dawn, a broken sight

Of blown-up flames, and tongues of fire that leap

And feast already on the fringe of night,

Singeing her very footsteps in the deep;—

Nay, by the thrones upon the steadfast tips

Of mountains, where the light already reigns.

Nay, by all omens and sweet auguries

Of day that wins and night that shrinks and wanes,

Of day that dawns and every star that dies,

And distant foaming steeds of ocean bringing

Strange golden gifts of amber to our sands;

Nay, by some voice that is already singing

A harvest song in all the labouring lands.

Faith is more vital, and a greater strength

In all our hearts; and though from mere beginning

We be so frail, a very prey to death,

Yet are we found, yea, we do think at length,

More than a mere wind ceasing, more than breath,

Great in great ends of perishing or winning.

In all of us alike this one hope thrills,

Ay more or less at heart: and these the strong,

Beholding very early from the hills,

Cry out; and we the weak lie still and long.

Come! for we are quite weary of the spaces

Between the nights that know thee not, and days

That dawn not, holding thee in solemn places

Suns soften not, nor yet with any strength

Of yearning or of crying we attain:

We are as stars all weary through the dark,

Holding inconstant vassalage in vain,

Till thou, our sun long tarrying—thou at length

Steering into our midst a perfect bark

Of day, shalt come with conquering to aid us.

We are no better than mere flowers groping

To die in light ;—we are the thing God made us ;

We live as all things trembling, all things hoping ;

We die as leaves that are consumed with fire,   .

And shades, we hunt some shade of our desire.

The far tops of the hills are lit with thee,

And melt with love of many distant lights

Down in the deep horizon of the sea

Dawning ; the very winds are still at nights

Waiting, and leaves are whispering of thee

All day ; and in the forest stirs a thunder

Fitfully, as of armies drawing near,

Distinctly as of hoofs and tramp of steeds ;

And echoes bring far sound of clarions clear :

Yea, all the world is full of hope and wonder :

Hail to the men and honour to the deeds !

Afar in dimness of long dreams beholden,

End of all hopes and tender prophecies,

Age, that art glorious—Age, that art all golden,

Hail ! we do yearn to touch thee with these eyes :

We, that shall evermore be dark and holden

Of night among mere shadows of things past,

Yearn for thee, stretching forth our souls and crying,

Save us, O saviour ! heal us, O our sun,

In these our lives ! or grant us even at last

To see thy glories in a vision, dying,—

Men that shall be, and deeds that shall be done.

SONG.

I N the long enchanted weather,
  When lovers came together,
And fields were bright with blossoming,
  And hearts were light with song;

When the poet lay for hours
In a dream among the flowers,
And heard a soft voice murmuring
  His love's name all day long;

Or for hours stood beholding
The summer time unfolding
Its casket of rich jewelries,
  And boundless wealth outpoured;

Saw the precious-looking roses

Its glowing hand uncloses,

The pearls of dew and emeralds

    Spread over grass and sward ;

When he heard besides the singing,

Mysterious voices ringing

With clear unearthly ecstasies

    Through earth and sky and air ;

Then he wondered for whose pleasure

Some king made all that treasure—

That bauble of the universe,

    At whose feet it was laid :

Yea, for what celestial leman,

Bright saint or crownèd demon,

Chimed all the tender harmonies

    Of that rich serenade.

But his heart constrained him, sinking

Back to its sweetest thinking,

His lady all to celebrate

And tell her beauty's worth;

And he sought at length what tender

Love-verses he should send her:

Oh, the love within him overflowed,

And seemed to fill the earth!

So he took, in his emotion,

A murmur from the ocean;

He took a plaintive whispering

Of sadness from the wind;

. And a piteous way of sighing

From the leaves when they were dying,

And the music of the nightingales

With all his own combined;

Yea, he stole indeed some phrases
Of mystic hymns of praises,
The heaven itself is perfecting
  Out of the earthly things ;

And with these he did so fashion
The poem of his passion,
The lady still is listening,
  And still the poet sings !

A FAREWELL.

HATH any loved you well down there,
  Summer or winter through?
Down there, have you found any fair
  Laid in the grave with you?
Is death's long kiss a richer kiss
  Than mine was wont to be?
Or have you gone to some far bliss,
  And quite forgotten me?

What soft enamouring of sleep
  Hath you in some soft way?
What charmed death holdeth you with deep
  Strange lure by night and day?

A little space below the grass,
 Out of the sun and shade ;
But worlds away from me, alas !
 Down there where you are laid !

My bright hair's waved and wasted gold,
 What is it now to thee
Whether the rose-red life I hold
 Or white death holdeth me ?
Down there you love the grave's own green,
 And evermore you rave
Of some sweet seraph you have seen
 Or dreamed of in the grave.

There you shall lie as you have lain,
 Though in the world above
Another live your life again,
 Loving again your love ;
Is it not sweet beneath the palm ?
 Is not the warm day rife

With some long mystic golden calm
    Better than love and life?

The broad quaint odorous leaves, like hands
    Weaving the fair day through,
Weave sleep no burnished bird withstands,
    While death weaves sleep for you ;
And many a strange rich breathing sound
    Ravishes morn and noon ;
And in that place you must have found
    Death a delicious swoon.

Hold me no longer for a word
    I used to say or sing ;
Ah ! long ago you must have heard
    So many a sweeter thing :
For rich earth must have reached your heart,
    And turned the faith to flowers ;
And warm wind stolen, part by part,
    Your soul through faithless hours.

And many a soft seed must have won
Soil of some yielding thought,
To bring a bloom up to the sun
That else had ne'er been brought;
And doubtless many a passionate hue
Hath made that place more fair,
Making some passionate part of you
Faithless to me down there.

EUROPE.

I AM young, and full of the earnestness of love ;
    And I seek some great faith wherein I may live,—
Some faith of youthful men who strive and move
And fight and win, while out of all they live ;
For well my heart is telling me—above
God changes not, and death will surely give
Him to thy soul ; therefore, with man now, live.

I go up, yea, all the heart within me singing,
To the golden crags, to the giant thrones of light ;
And through blue gloom I see the young day clinging
To reluctant folds of the slowly vanishing night.

So a man's heart clings maybe to an old faith dying :

But I—I must have some faith that will not die ;

Not of the faiths that end in dreaming and sighing,

Which a man gives up at the last with a dismal cry.

Would that from yonder mountain's height, alone—

The sun just crowns it—I could see the day,—

The young, the strong day, the day that shall be my
       own,—

Grow and roll over the world with conquering sway!

Would I might see indeed earth's many lands,

And nations rising, and nations passing away,

And which faith fails, and which it is that withstands,

And then, bounding all, the waste sea and the sands !

For oh ! my heart is strong, and the world is weak ;

Yet the world is doing the master-work I seek ;

And workers, ay, and hinderers, are but blind,

Building new or destroying what they find ;

And I would be with the workers in the van ;

For somehow, somewhere, rises god-like Man.

O fallen France ! the sun floods over you :

I look upon you—I, sometime your lover.

It was a soft delicious song that drew

My heart : it was the roses that soon cover

The heaped - up graves where recently men
    threw

Mere fameless earth over most famous men :

It was the rose I saw, the song I heard,

That lured me, till I thought I loved you. Then,

Fair courtesan, I found you ; and the learning

Of many a precious fantasy and word

Of rare unalterable magic, turning

The dreary wastes of life to flowering ways,

Lies treasured in my heart. You seemed awhile

To reign there rose-crowned, fronting full the rays

Of coming summers and of dawning days,

With luminous foreknowledge in your smile ;

And all your poets, singing lofty song,

Stood gleaming where the clouds of morning
    part,

Leading, it seemed, fair lines of men along,—

Leading each man by something in his heart

On to the radiant future.   Then, what wonder

That, while your fascinating semblance held

Man's soul in men like those, your fair lips spelled

And uttered softly, and it grew to thunder,

Acclaimed by the believing human race,

The lofty language of man's soul—the thing

He dreams of, and he sees as yon pure vision

Of shapely cloud, now like a young god's face,

Now an ideal bark, now with vast wing

Chimerical, albeit far, elysian,—

A thing to be, but not embodied yet

In element of earth—the golden state,

The last man's Eden, which the gods have set,

Methinks, beyond too many a bloody gate—

The thing men call Republic ?

                              Rang once more

The lifted music of that golden theme

From those too sanguine singers ; from the shore

Of the world's far unrealisable dream,

Yea, from that distant and receding day

Of godlike consummation, which I pray

Dawn on the final finished rest of man,

Floated forth once again the angelic dove

Whose name is Peace, to seek her fellow, Love ;

For whom not yet, nor since the world began,

Is one fair spot wherein to make abode.

Yea, France, your poets nobly thought and sang

A holy and regenerating ode ;

And you, with ribald clamour and harsh clang

Of common tongues, and brass, and bloody swords,

Set about founding to those soaring words

The low, inane, the grovelling mockery

Which you conceived, which was the thing their
    light

Begot in your brute bosom.   And I, maybe

Catching the echo, breathing the delight

Of most exalted music hither blown
With wafts of perfume from a foreign land,
Gazed for a little on your face, soon grown
Aptly transfigured, with some faining bland
Masking its low-aimed glance and paltry scope,
And waited for a while 'twixt fear and hope.
Then came upon me the discordant tone
Of vulgar untuned voices.　As I gaze,
Vile crowds, a populace, your men, your own,
Polluted France! burst forth with hideous praise
Responding to your call; the paltry shout
Of each besotted individual voice;
The senseless swaying of that rabble rout;
Base sheddings of base blood; villainous choice
Of most defenceless victims to bear death
For some abjured sin when the sin's shamed out;
The cursings, strivings, hootings—one that saith
This way is Peace, another, Strike this way
For Liberty; and all some self to place
Upon some puny pinnacle for a day!

What is all this but the unholy seething

Of fierce defilers of the human race

Whose country is a brothel?

                  Where the while

Are those most lofty poets whose souls, breathing

Some upper air, dwelling in some rare smile,

Forecast of sweet futurity, were holding

Enraptured converse with man's godlike dreams,

That walk indeed as men in godlike moulding,

Nigh the world's end, where perfect morning gleams?

Them had that clamorous multitude first hailed

As even the high priests of the coming shame,

The common scandal called by their great name :

Where are thy poets now?   They once prevailed,

O France ! to make thee seem before mankind

A beauteous vision of a foremost land,

Leading on towards the dawn.   No man shall find

Their names at all with thine in after time,

Dull tottering Republic.   Lone and grand,

One, from a lifelong exile by the sea

Returning, lives an exile still in thee,

His soul for ever in his dream sublime !

And One is dead—alas ! 'tis even He

Who was the priest of beauty.

　　　　　　　　　　　　Since no singing

Hath come across thy stained wave, ever bringing

Most hideous jarring echoes of the strife

Of such vile folk as do degrade man's life,

With maybe some corrupt imagining,

Degenerate offspring of the loathsome gloom

And damp distorted glimmer of thy tomb.

Lie there, for thou wilt never rise or sing

Perchance again ; and in my life's own time

Thou 'lt be for nought : I turn from thy harsh
　　　noise

And sullen degradation.

　　　　　　　　　　　　Still, sublime,

I feel within—as though I heard a voice,

Unaltered prophesying—all the thought,

The great eternal thought, that makes most great

This palpitating human life,—the thought

Of the supreme fruitions that await

The strong progressive rising soul of man

In the fair end of time.   Since time began,

Each separate sun makes one short day, and
    sets ;

But onward time descends not, nor forgets

The long ascent to high eternity :

And so, man falls away, and man is lost,

And nations sink into obscurity ;

But the sure bark that holds humanity

Rides far ahead, on other waters tost,

Triumphing forward.

                Where the soul, undying,

Ethereally forms or finishes

Man's new undying body, culturing

Each flower of man's dreaming or man's sighing,

Each delicate germ of thoughts that were scarce his,

But for each warmer summer his heart may bring

To rear the plant whose every tendril is

An aspiration—there I seek to sing ;

Yea, that shall be my country, and the king

Shall be the king, and I a singer there,

For there 'twill soon be heaven.

             The great dawn grows

In glittering Germany, no flower of mere

Forced loveliness, or transient, but the rose

Whose rich futurity of summers redden

In the strong conscious storehouse of the heart.

And there while somewhat of man's soul all hidden

Progresses warily through fertile shade

To timely day, already some fair part

Hath preluded in music that hath made

The world once more rebuild the shrines of art.

But Russia rises, and the freed folk learn

The higher freedom of man's heart from songs

Ancient but unforgotten, which return

Across the songless waste of dismal wrongs,

To find the heart of man can rise and yearn,

And sing forever.   Lo ! the Kremlin's towers

Catch the clear icy radiance of the dawn.

All the North wears a crown of frozen flowers;

While southward, among lands that with green

    lawn

And vine-field slope down seaward where the

    sea

Is that blue Mediterranean, whose warm kiss

Woos them and enervates them; Italy,

Spoiled, nerveless offspring of great centuries,

Lies fretting in rich rags of luxury.

While, checking colder waves that own her sway,

Insular England, sitting aye aloof

Behind closed door, and under jealous roof,

Resistful of new suns that dawn to day

Is letting in, well seen, and put to proof,

The world's full yesterday.

　　　　　　　　So while I look,

The lands gleam slowly forth before my soul,

And there is gradual growth that will not brook

The heaping up and clogging of the past ;

And while I look, far doors of morning roll

Grandly apart, as with some onward blast,

And saffron thresholds of the future cast

Their radiance hither, even o'er my soul.

And to me, with love's earnestness desiring

To see some foremost banner with the name

Of　mankind's　foremost　faith　wrought　like　a

　　　flame,

That I might go up all my life aspiring,

There seems now in the morning a clear sight,

A thing scarce dream-like—not again one land

Crowned and transcendant leading for a space

A little way the nations into light,

But a more splendid vision, as of grand

Unanimous Europe, lifting up a face

That none hath seen till now—a face whose glory

Is made indeed of every nation's story,

Whose smile is full of all their pasts, whose brow

Is busy with the problems of their Now,

But whose transcendant look already glows

In lofty futures that no man yet knows.

That vision rises : in this early morn,

When time is, even as I, a thing new-born,

That vision rises, from the uncertain haze,

A faint foreshadowing of the future days,

Ethereal, seen of few.   Maybe vast Rome

Stands yet clear grandeur in the eastern fire,

And France looks shapely still in strange attire ;

But my young soul knows, in this faithless morn,

France is already fallen, and mightier Rome

There in the glow is but a hollow dome

Now tottering.   So this Europe is my creed,

Its boundless future shall shape forth and lead

My soul in search of morning ; I and they,

Whose lives shall run with my life from to-day,

With all our earnest might of thought and deed

We will be joined to strive to that great end,

Seen clearly,—as the higher than that which is,

The goal of all in man that still must tend

Upward, and never halt at such as this,

Which is half-light, or this some short-lived best,

The heaping up of ruined yesterdays ·

Against to-morrow's sunrise.   They who rest

Under the most consummate roof they raise

Shall surely lie beneath its overthrow ;

But I and some in all the lands will go

Onward for ever singing : every song

Shall help and urge our armies' feet along ;

And no land's straitened law shall judge the thing

We do, for that we do and that we sing

Shall come to nought for ever, or have might,

Where human Europe moves from light to light.

PRINTED BY BALLANTYNE AND COMPANY
EDINBURGH AND LONDON

AN EPIC OF WOMEN,

And Other Poems.

By ARTHUR O'SHAUGHNESSY.

WITH SOME ORIGINAL DESIGNS BY MR J. T. NETTLESHIP.

The Academy.—" Influences to which we should be inclined to refer it are those of a section of the French Romantiques, Baudelaire and Gautier at their head, who set themselves, with a conscious purpose of art, and with an immense care for the technical execution, finish, and symmetry of their art, to give expression to remote phases of super-subtle feeling or perverse imagination, to produce fantastic and demoralised spiritual exotics of the finest colour and perfume. . . . There is finished writing in all of them (Mr O'S.'s poems). . . . Of the formal art of poetry he is in many senses quite a master; his metres are not only good, they are his own, and often of an invention most felicitous as well as careful."

P

Athenæum.—"We have no hesitation in avowing our conviction that the volume before us is a work that raises high expectations, and were we sure that the faults we observe in him are due to inexperience, and not the result of his own nature, we should predict for Mr O'Shaughnessy great success in the future. . . . With its quaint title and quaint illustrations, 'An Epic of Women' will be a rich treat to a wide circle of admirers. . . . Mr O'Shaughnessy has obviously attempted to deal with the two elements of our nature, spirit and matter. . . . 'Cleopatra' is a fine poem. The picture of the Queen in the first stanza is remarkably beautiful. Among the poems not to be omitted from mention are 'A Whisper from the Grave,' and 'The Fountain of Tears,' noticeable for the fine roll of its rhythm. This we should like to quote in its entirety."

Examiner.—"There is a wild sublimity of imagery in these poems. . . . Many of his verses are exceedingly beautiful. . . . They are like a delicious melody that enchants the ear and leaves an impression on the sense after the sound has died away. The metrical formation, too, is generally marked by elegance and accuracy, while the rhymes are easy and graceful."

Sunday Times.—"The book before us seems to announce the advent of a new poet, and one adequate to take part in the concert of modern singers. There are in the work before us freshness, spontaneity, and fervour, such as generally mark the possession of the divine afflatus."

Weekly Despatch.—"A distinguished living critic has pronounced this author to be another Morris. . . . There is no doubt that this is a book of the highest class. . . . But it is almost too good for our busy day, when reading leisure is so scarce. It suggests at once some sunny Ionian isle, not omitting the Ionian dances, and the Ionian wine. Of its school it is by far the best book we have met with for a long time."

Illustrated London News.—"Mr O'Shaughnessy is not merely a young writer of genuine poetic feeling, but his poems in general possess the ease and finish of the accomplished artist. They are usually perfect wholes,— a result the more remarkable when viewed in connection with the affluence of his lyrical faculty, and the apparent spontaneity of his inspiration."

Manchester Guardian.—"As we lay down this book, there remains a 'singing in the ear,'—a singing original, clear, melodious. . . . That his inspiration manifests itself in a truly original mode we shall show by illustration ; that all the book bears proofs of genius our readers will perhaps believe on our word. . . . We welcome such a singer as a genuine addition to the bardic circle which holds our faith."

Court Circular.—"To the taste and culture which characterise the more eminent of modern writers of verse Mr O'Shaughnessy adds a lyrical faculty and command of music unequalled, except in one or two supreme singers. . . . Not a weak or meaningless

composition disfigures a work almost as admirable
for its symmetry as a whole, as for the rare value
of individual poems. . . . In their general scope, in
the aspirations they convey, and the experiences they
record, they stand apart and alone."

From "Our Living Poets," by H. Buxton Forman.—
"There is not here any of the rampant viciousness we
have seen in some recent poetry, but rather what should
seem to be an accidental cynicism, sure to pass away
with a few years of work as noble in manner as Mr O'S.
promises to do. It seems almost a matter of course that
a young poet, of a highly ideal and sensuous tendency,
should feel something of a bitter isolation in these days
of realistic and colourless outward existence. In like
manner, it is not surprising that one who shows so
delicate a sense of material beauty should have been
overwhelmed by the consideration that so many of the
traditional queens of beauty did very little good in the
world, and a great deal of harm. Some day, perhaps,
Mr O'S. will give us splendid poetry, showing a sense
that woman's fairness is no such baneful thing when its
influences are judged justly and widely ; but at present
we may accept the poems of the so-called 'Epic of
Women,' with a keen sense of the extraordinary strength
and directness they own as first lyric qualities. . . . It
is justifiable to select 'The Daughter of Herodias,' and
record one's opinion that here is a work of sufficient beauty
and scope and truth to remove the author from the ranks

of mere scholar-poets, and give him at once the unquali-
fied standing of a poet. . . . The two stanzas given below
seem to me to be truly grand. Of Mr O'S.'s smaller
poems, the three most pleasing are ' A Whisper from the
Grave,' 'The Fountain of Tears,' and 'The Spectre of the
Past ;' these three are perfectly clear in their pathetic
meaning, and notably excellent in metric and rhythmic
qualities. Indeed, as regards the invention and use of
metres the author is particularly happy. Those of his
own originating are, at the same time, simple, musical,
and individual ; . . . and it seems probable that, as years
go on, he will have that to tell to men which will be
well worth the garment of a perfect poetic manner of
speech."

. . . And Mr O'S. is also an accomplished master in those peculiar turns of rhythm which are designed to reproduce the manner of the mediæval originals."

Home Journal (American.)—"Foremost among the younger poets is Arthur O'S. He is thoroughly original ; his versification is polished though far from laboured ; his expression of thought peculiarly clear and distinct. Altogether we may hail him as a true genius, and as such, heartily welcome him to a prominent place in the literary ranks of English poets."

Sunday Times.—"The merit of Mr O'S.'s first volume of poems, 'An Epic of Women,' was such that the early appearance of another work from the same pen became a matter of keen interest to lovers of poetry. Mr O'S. has treated his subjects boldly, with the touch of a master."

Examiner.—"His themes are old-fashioned, but the phrases in which he portrays them are altogether modern. . . . The way in which it is told goes far to make it better than anything else that Mr O'S. has written. Mr O'S. vastly improves upon Marie's lay in his description of the growth of Guilliadun's pure and honest love, so pure and honest that it innocently betrays itself to Eliduc, and of Eliduc's gradual yielding of himself to her fascinations in despite of his duty to his wife."